GOOD FRIEND, what Matter how or whence you come
To walk these Streets which are the Nation's Home;
Rest for a Time and—resting—read herein,
Seek from the Past and—seeking—Wisdom win:
For if the Things you see give you no Gain,
The LIVES of many MEN were lived in vain.

A Likeneſs of His Majeſty, King William III, in whoſe
Honour the City of Williamſburg in Virginia was
named. Now newly made, by E. Jones
after an ancient Engraving.

A
BRIEF & TRUE REPORT
CONCERNING
Williamsburg
in VIRGINIA:

*Being an Account of the most important
Occurrences in that Place from its
first Beginning to the present Time.*

AND containing precisely the same Text
(now newly set in modern Types) which
appeared in the enlarged and revised Third
Edition — but without the Appendix of
two Hundred and thirty-two Pages by
which the Text of the Third Edition was
fully annotated.

By *RUTHERFOORD GOODWIN*,
An Inhabitant *of the* Place.

𝕬 𝕱ourth & 𝕬bridged 𝕰dition

WILLIAMSBURG:
Printed for *Colonial Williamsburg*, Incorporated,
by *August Dietz* and his Son on their Press in
Cary Street at *Richmond, Virginia.* MCM,XLI.

A
PREFACE
TO THE
READER.

THE First Edition *of* "Williamsburg in Virginia" *appeared as an official Publication of the* Williamsburg Restoration *in 1935, when the Restoration had been in Progress above eight Years and when it was believed to be nearing Completion.*

Since that Time the Scope and Scale of the Project have been altered and extended, as have subsequent Editions of this Book. Therefore, to the Readers of this Fourth *and abridged Edition, certain Facts concerning the Variations of the several Editions should be made plain.*

[iii]

The first two Editions, appearing in 1935 and 1936, contained, in addition to the Text, a Division for guiding Visitors to Buildings and Sites of especial Interest in Williamsburg, which Division was composed principally of brief Sketches concerning the individual Histories of such Places. Intended, then, to serve the dual Purpose of historical Outline and Guidebook, the Volumes were designed after the Manner of the rude Travel Books of the colonial Period. Caslon Types and early Ornaments were employed, these being Hand-set in keeping with ancient Printers' Forms, and including the Letters and Ligatures (ſ, ſſ, ſb, ſi, ſk, ſl, ſſi, ſſl, and &) which also characterized the Publications of Williamsburg's colonial Printers. In the Preparation of the Text the more commonplace Phraseology of the Period was emulated, and contemporary Inelegancies of Style were advisedly introduced.

The Third Edition (issued in February 1941), differs markedly from its Predecessors and also from this present Volume. On the

Basis of Experience gained from previous Editions, and in View of the continued Expansion of the Restoration both in the Construction of Buildings and in historical Research concerning them, it had proved more practical to entrust Guide Information to Publications of less permanent Character. In Consequence, the Division for Guiding was not included in the Third Edition. In its Place an unusually extensive Appendix was added, which increased the Length from two Hundred Pages to four Hundred and sixteen Pages. This Appendix provides a complete Annotation of the Text, interspersed with pertinent Quotations from the Works and Sources consulted. It also contains true Copies of the Acts passed by the General Assembly of Virginia in 1699, 1701, and 1705 for directing the Building of the City of Williamsburg and the Capitol, as well as the Text of the City's Charter of 1722. Altered in Purpose and larger in Size, the Third Edition was re-designed and re-set after the Manner of the *more ambitious Works of* Williamsburg's *colonial Printers — notably the* "History of the First Discovery and Settlement of Virginia," *by* William Stith, *A. M., which was printed and bound at* Williamsburg *by* William Parks *in 1747, and was the first History of* Virginia *to be printed in* Virginia. *Again individual Types were employed, including the archaic Letters, Ligatures, and Ornaments of the early Printers. The Books were printed on special Paper which, though Machine-made, closely resembles the Hand-made Products of* William Parks' *Paper Mill — the first Mill of its Kind in the* South — *which was established in* Williamsburg *about 1744. In this Edition all practicable Means, including Hand-forwarded Bindings in full Leather, were resorted to in an Effort to produce Books which, while outlining the History of the City and its Restoration, would exemplify as closely as possible these fundamental Crafts and Industries of its Past.*

The Fourth Edition *(and this present*

Volume) varies in a Number of Respects from those previously produced. The Guide Division of the first two Editions has been eliminated. The extensive Appendix of the Third Edition *is not included. With this Exception, the Text is precisely the same as that of the* Third Edition, *and it may be reassuring to the Reader to know that the Statements made herein are substantiated by Citation or Quotation, or by both, in the Appendix contained in the Volumes of the* Third Edition.

In Format the present Volume is reminiscent and, in many Ways, indicative of Publications produced in Williamsburg *in the Eighteenth Century. The Type, however, is "Machine* Caslon," *and the archaic "long S," together with the Ligatures which accompany it, is thus necessarily eliminated. The Book-paper is identical with that used in the* Third Edition. *The Cover Paper is copied from an old Paper and is late Eighteenth Century in Character.*

Finally, it should be noted that the Quo-

tations appearing *in* the *Text* are *capital-ized and italicized in keeping with the typo-graphic Style of this Book. They are other-wise true Copies in every Respect. The Appendix in the Volumes of the* Third Edition *will afford a detailed Record of their Sources.*

R. G.

WILLIAMSBURG, VIRGINIA

April, 1941.

A TABLE

OF THE

CONTENTS.

CHAPTER I.

CHAPTER II.

ILLUSTRATIONS.

[xi]

Signing of an Agreement of Non-importation, or, else, the Loyalists forced to such an Association by the Sentiment of the Public.

Facing p. 65.

7. A Map of the City of *Williamsburg*, engraved in the Year 1940, after a Drawing made in 1782 by an unknown *French* Cartographer.

Facing p. 112.

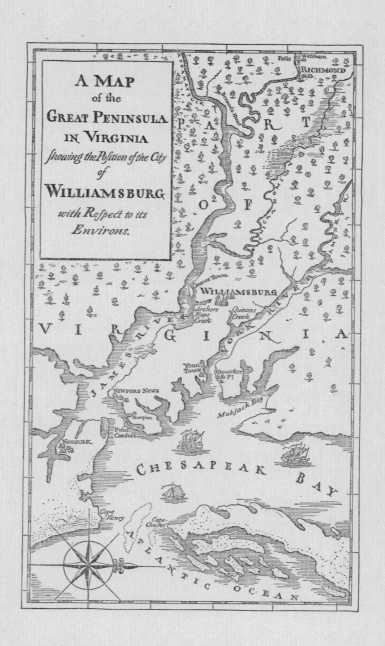

A MAP
of the
GREAT PENINSULA
IN VIRGINIA
shewing the Position of the City
of
WILLIAMSBURG
with Respect to its
Environs.

A BRIEF & TRUE REPORT

CONCERNING

WILLIAMSBURG
in VIRGINIA

CHAPTER I.

ILLIAMSBURG, which was known at its first Beginning as *Middle Plantation,* was born in the Year 1633 out of those dreadful Misgivings which oppressed the Settlers that first dwelt in the *Virginia* Colony.

SOME Years previous to this Time, in 1622, the heathen *Indians,* doubtless thinking themselves well justified by the Encroachment of the *English,* had contrived and perpetrated the most barbarous Massacre, wherein near one Third of all the Inhabitants of the Colony were cruelly slain. And it was this grievous Occurrence which brought about the Raising of Palisades across the Peninsula between the Rivers *York* and *James*. The Raising of such Palisades, in its Turn, occasioned the Establishment of a Settlement which, perhaps because it centered upon the Ridge of the Peninsula and filled the Space that was between the newly seated Plantations on the *York* River and the older Plantations on the *James* River, or perhaps because it was established within the Space between two Palisades, was called *Middle Plantation*.

FROM the meager Records of those Times it appears that the general Purpose was this: That Fortifications of Pales (that is of Logs planted endwise) should be built across the exposed Breadth of the Peninsula, and that between the Palisades there should be a continued Succession of inhabited Lands. With this Front presented to the *Indians,* it was further purposed to maintain a Guard upon the Palisades and to exclude all *Indians* and *Indian* Habitations from the East of them, in Order that the Settlers in the lower End of the Peninsula might labour unguarded in their Fields, and that their Children, their Servants, their Cattle, and their Swine might go in some Assurance of their Lives.

THUS it was that at a Grand Assembly of the Burgesses and the Council "holden at *James Citty* "[*Jamestown*] the first Day of *February, 1632/3,*" at which Sir *John Harvey* sat as Governor, an Act was passed entitled *An Act for the Seatinge of the Middle Plantation.* And this Act, in the Words which follow, ordered:

[2]

"That every fortyeth Man be chosen and
"maynteyned out of the tithable Persons of all the
"Inhabitants, within the Compasse of the Forrest
"conteyned betweene *Queenes* Creeke in *Charles*
"River [meaning either *York* River or *Charles*
"*River* County, afterwards the County of *York*],
"and *Archers Hope* Creeke in *James* River, with
"all the Lands included, to the Bay of *Chesepiake*,
"and it is appoynted that the sayd Men be there
"at the Plantation of Doct. *John Pott,* newlie built
"before the first Day of *March* next, and that
"the Men be imployed in buildinge of Houses, and
"securinge that Tract of Land lyinge betweene the
"sayd Creekes. And to doe such other Workes as
"soone as may bee, as may defray the Chardges
"of that Worke, and to be directed therein as they
"shall be ordered by the Governor and Counsell.
"And yf any free Men shall this Yeare before the
"first Day of *May,* voluntarilie goe and seate
"uppon the sayd Place of the *Middle Plantation,*
"they shall have fifty Acres of Land Inheritance,
"and be free from all Taxes and publique Chardges
"according to a former Act of Assembly made the
"forth Day of *September* last past."

A N D it should be well observed by the Reader
that the Plantation, ordered and encouraged by
this Act, was a Planting of Men in a Settlement,
rather than the Seating of a single Planter. The
Reader, on the other Hand, should not be misled
to picture *Middle Plantation* in his Mind, as some
have done, as a Town to be compared with the
Towns of this present Day, nor even as a Town in
the Sense that *Jamestown* was a Town in that early
Day. More Truth will be found in looking upon
it as a wide-scattered Settlement in which no Man

had Need to be disturbed by the Wailing of his Neighbor's Offspring; yet which, with the Years, converged upon a middle Point until, of a Sudden, it became a City—as shall be told in its proper Time and Place. ❄ ❄ ❄

THE History of the early Years of *Middle Plantation* is, in great Part, hidden in Obscurity; for in those Times all Men were, to a surprising Extent, Soldiers and Labourers in a common Cause, even while they sought their own Prosperity and Advancement. In this Wise the History of the Part did frequently become lost in the History of the Whole; and the Admission should be made that even Facts of Interest pertaining to the whole Country have in many Instances been lost in the Advance and Destruction of Time, and must now be supplied from Speculation.

YET, it would seem that as soon as 1634 the Settlement had its Commander, one *Richard Popeley*; and it would appear that in 1646, after the *Indians* had risen in their second great Massacre in the Year 1644, *Middle Plantation* had become of such a Consequence that Captain *Robert Higginson* was appointed to erect a new Pale at that Place or, it may be, to repair the old one. Nor was the Service of *God* neglected there, for a Parish was early established, which, in 1658, was united with *Harrop* Parish to form *Middletowne* Parish; and this Parish, in its Turn, was united in 1674 with *Marston* Parish to form *Bruton* Parish, which last survives to this present Day.

[4]

The Great Massacre in the Colony of VIRGINIA, in the Year 1622.
From a fine Engraving by Theodore de Bry.

AND in these Years there were many of every Rank who patented Land in *Middle Plantation.* The first among them, who indeed was seated before the Settlement, was Doctor *John Pott,* the Physician General of the Colony, a Man in whom there was a great Conflict of Virtue and Mischief; for, though he had served as the Governor of *Virginia* in the Year 1629, yet in 1630 he was tried and convicted of stealing Cattle; and, though he was held to be the foremost Physician of the Country and the only one that could be said to be "skilled in Epidemical Diseases," yet was he equally renowned for his Appetite for strong Waters and low Company "who hung upon him "while his good Liquor lasted." And, again, though he had himself been Governor, he was a prominent Member of the Council which, in 1635, thrust Sir *John Harvey* out of his Governorship and sent him Home to his Sovereign.

AMONG the many others, less confused in their Dispositions than this Doctor *Pott,* who settled at *Middle Plantation,* were *Edward* and *George Wyatt,* Nephews of Sir *Francis Wyatt,* who was twice Governor of *Virginia; Henry Tyler,* the Ancestor to President *John Tyler; Richard Kempe,* who was made Secretary of the Colony by Sir *John Harvey; Robert Higginson* of the " an- " cient Family of the *Higginsons,*" known as " the " Valliant Captain *Robert Higginson.* One of the " first Command'rs that subdued the Country of " *Virginia* from the Power of the Heathen ";

[5]

Thomas Ludwell, who was also Secretary of the Colony; Major *Otho Thorpe*, whose Kinsman, *George Thorpe*, had been a great and devoted Friend to the *Indians* and had been killed by them in the Massacre of 1622; Colonel *John Page*, a Member of the Council; *James Bray*, also a Member of the Council; and many others of like and less Distinction. Thus, it will be seen that the Settlement, even in its first forty Years, was not without Standing in the Colony, nor without Influence in its Governance.

❀ ❀ ❀

BY the Year 1676, *Middle Plantation* had come to be recognized as " the very Heart and " Centre of the Country," and had gained an Importance second only to that of *Jamestown*. And in that Year it gained further Distinction and Prominence when it became, to some Degree, the Heart and Centre of a great Revolt of the People; which was led by *Nathaniel Bacon*, Jr., and which, though it began as a March against the heathen Savages, yet ended in an open War against the tyrannical Misdoings of Sir *William Berkeley*, the King's Governor.

THE Causes of *Bacon's Rebellion* were of many varying Sorts, and in this brief Space it can only be recited that, on Account of the low Ebb of Tobacco Prices, the Times were exceeding poor; yet the Taxes were daily and mightily increased for the Enrichment of the *Grandees* who surrounded the

Governor, for the Support of a weak and biased Assembly which the Governor had held in Office for some fourteen Years, for the Cost of Opposition to the Proprietorship into which the King had been pleased to grant away the whole Colony, and for the Erection and Maintaining of Forts which the People considered small Protection. And upon a People already thus distressed and burdened the *Indian* Infidels fell daily with their Murderings and Maraudings in the outlying Places, yet met with small Censure and less Opposition from the Governor; which some may have thought was because he feared a War with them, but others said was because he loved them too well, he having a prosperous private Trade with them in Beaver Skins.

So it was that the People, despairing of Protection from those that governed them, began without Authority to " beat up Drums for Volunteers to " goe out against the *Indians* " and to draw into Arms. And soon they had for their Leader this *Bacon*, a Gentleman of great Figure and Prominence in the Country, who, though he was a young Man, yet was born to lead other Men and to inspire their Spirit with his Words.

TWICE *Bacon* led an Army against the Savages; at the first in Defiance of Sir *William Berkeley*, and, in the second Instance, with a Commission as General of all the Forces in *Virginia* against the *Indians*, which he had forced from the Governor and the Assembly with a great Show of Arms. Yet

[7]

on each Occasion he and those that followed him were proclaimed Rebels and Mutineers by the Governor, who sought to raise Men to put them down. Thus, *Bacon* was brought to see that if he would go out against the *Indians*, he must first go against those that he sought to protect; and so he reversed his March to give them Battle.

RETURNED from the Frontier, *Bacon* found that the Governor, having been deserted by most of those he had raised to fight the Rebels, had fled into *Accomac* County on the eastern Shore of the *Chesapeake*. And, so, finding himself embroiled in a civil War against the King's Regent, he quartered his Troops at *Middle Plantation* and summoned all the People of the Colony " of what " Quality soever, excepting Servants," to meet with him there. And when a great Company of People, including many of the principal Men of the Country, had come together in that Place, *Bacon* proposed an Oath to them by which, according to one of the Times, they should swear:

" First, to be aideing, with their Lives and
" Estates, the Generall, in the *Indian* War; second-
" ly, to oppose Sir *William's* Designes, if hee had
" any, to hinder the same; and, lastly, to protect
" the Generall, Army and all that should subscribe
" to this Ingagement, against any Power that
" should be sent out of *England,* till it should be
" granted that the Country's Complaint might be
" heard against Sr. *William* before the King and
" Parliament."

And in Defense of this Oath, which some feared,

[8]

Bacon argued that five Hundred *Virginians* might beat two Thousand Red Coats, and he further stated that he would resign his Commission to the Assembly if the Oath should be refused; and so there were few that refused it.

N O W *Bacon*, having the Support of near the whole Country, marched out a third Time against the *Indians*; but he found his chosen Adversaries exceeding scarce, they having hidden themselves in the Swamps or fled to other Parts through Fear of him. And, as he pursued them, he learned that *Berkeley* had returned out of *Accomac* with a considerable Following from that Quarter, and had taken *Jamestown* and fortified it. Then, with his customary Dispatch and Boldness, *Bacon* marched upon *Jamestown* and laid a Siege there; and, after many brave and strange Happenings, *Berkeley* discovered that his Supporters were as fickle in their Loyalty as *Bacon's* Men were strong in theirs, and so, with those that were true to him, he fled again into *Accomac*. And immediately *Bacon* entered into the Town and burned it into an Heap of Ashes that " the Rogues," as he said, " should harbour " no more there."

A T the Height of his Power, *Bacon* now moved into *Gloucester* County, and there he laid many promising Plans for the Furthering of the *Indian* War; the Pursuit of *Berkeley* into *Accomac*; the general Ordering and Relief of the Country; and, if Need be, the Resistance of the armed Force of a Thousand Red Coats that had been sent against him out of *England*. But, as one Story of the Times has told it, *Bacon*, having destroyed *Jamestown*, was himself destroyed by *Jamestown*; for a great Fever, taken in the Swamps in the Siege of that Place, came upon him and, Fate being stronger than Man, he surrendered to it and died. And it is a true Measure of the Strength and Power of the Man that, upon his Death, the Rebellion he had led sputtered like a Candle Flame and went out.

I N an amazing small Space of Time Sir *William Berkeley* came again into full Control of the Government, and, in a vengeful Fury, he set about to hang all of the principal Followers of *Bacon* that came to his Hands. Some, including *William Drummond*, who had been Governor of *North Carolina*, he hanged at *Middle Plantation*; and yet others he hanged at *Green Spring*, his own country Estate. And a few, among whom were *Richard Lawrence*, *Thomas Whaley*, and *John Forth*, fled away into the Forests with their Arms, and were never heard of again; though some have supposed that they made their Way into *New England*, they preferring Life in that Climate to Death upon a Gallows. So that when the King's Troops arrived from *England* there was Nothing left for them to do in putting down the Revolt; but for the three Commissioners who came in charge of them, and to inquire into the whole Affair, there was much to do. And when the Commissioners set about to restore Tranquility in the tortured Colony, *Berkeley*, who could not bear that Peace and Prosperity should be spread among his Enemies, crossed them at every Turn. In the End he was recalled, and, leaving one of the Commissioners, Colonel *Herbert Jeffreys*, in his Place as Governor, he sailed for *England* in the Year 1677, and there he soon died.

THUS ended *Bacon's* Rebellion. And the Cause for being so particular in the Description of these Things should be plain: For not only did *Middle Plantation* have a prominent Part in all this melancholy Business, but also out of it, in devious Ways, came many of those Conditions which brought about the Upbuilding of the City of *Williamsburg* at *Middle Plantation*; for in those Times the Soil of *Virginia* was more suited to the Growth of Tobacco than it was to the Growth of Cities, and one City might grow only from the Strength and Fertility gained from Ashes of another. Nor was this Rebellion a Matter of small Concern and Consequence, as some ill-informed Persons have supposed; for though *Bacon's* Cause was lost upon the Field, yet many of its Principles and Purposes were won, and it is not beyond Reason to find in these Happenings the Planting of Seeds which were to blossom forth in later Times. ✿ ✿ ✿

WITH Peace restored to the Colony, yet with *Jamestown* lying in Ruin, *Middle Plantation* now served for a brief Space of Time as the Seat of Government. In *October*, 1677, a Grand Assembly was held there at the House of Captain *Otho Thorpe*, at which Assembly Acts were made for the Relief of the Country and a Proclamation from the King was read which pardoned all those that were engaged in the late Disturbance, *Bacon* himself being alone excepted (though, by Reason of the previous hasty Actions of *Berkeley*, there were many who lay beyond the Aid of this Pardon, unless its Words were to be carved upon their Gravestones). Also in this Year the King's Soldiers were quartered at *Middle Plantation*, and Governor *Jeffreys* summoned the chief Men of all the neighboring *Indian* Nations to come to the Camp there to treat about a lasting Peace. And with a great Show of Ceremony it was agreed that the *Indians* should live in Submission to the *English* and should be guaranteed good Treatment by them.

ABOUT this Time certain Inhabitants of *York* County filed a Petition with the King's Commissioners in which they entered the following Supplication:

" . . . And if a Towne be built for the Govnor
" Councell, Assembly to meet and for the Generall
" Court we humbly propose the *Middle Plantation*
" as thought the most fitt Place being the Center of
" the Country as alsoe within Land most safe from
" any fforeigne Enemy by Shipping, any Place upon
" a River Side being liable to the Battery of their
" greatt Guns."

YET *Jamestown* was still held in Favour and the State House was ordered to be rebuilt there;

though it is probable that the Place itself never again enjoyed the Size and Prominence it formerly had.

BUT in the Year 1693 a great Distinction did fall to *Middle Plantation*, for at that Time, their Majesties having been pleased to grant a Charter for the Founding of a College to be known in their Honour as the College of *William and Mary* in *Virginia*, the Assembly, having investigated several likely Locations, found *Middle Plantation* to be the most convenient and proper for that Design. In Consequence, it was enacted:

" . . . That *Middle Plantation* be the Place for " erecting the said College of *William and Mary* in " *Virginia* and that the said College be at that " Place erected and built as neare the Church now " standing in *Middle Plantation* old Fields as Con- " venience will permitt."

AND it should be mentioned that the Founding of the College grew in good Part from the Fervour and Labours of the Reverend Dr. *James Blair*, a young *Scotch* Clergyman in the Colony, who having suggested and furthered the Design in *Virginia*, was sent to *England* by the Assembly to promote the Plan at Court. And there he secured not only the Charter, but also a generous Endowment from the Crown; to which he added considerable Sums raised from private Persons, including certain Pirates whom he found in Prison and who were desirous of their Freedom. And so the Foundation Bricks of the principal College Building were laid in the Year 1695 under the Direction of Mr. *Thomas Hadley*, a Master Builder, who had been brought from *England* to fulfill the Plans which had been prepared in that Country by Sir *Christopher Wren*, the Surveyor General to their Majesties (he who drew the Plans for *St. Paul's* Cathedral in *London*).

A N D there are some who have sought to trace the Inspiration of the College to the University at *Henrico* that was proposed for *Virginia* in the Year 1618, and thus to advance it as the earliest College in all the Colonies. Yet, since the Design for the University at *Henrico* was defeated by the great Massacre of 1622 and by the Dissolution of the *Virginia* Company (by which Company the University was proposed), and moreover, since the proposed University was seated in another Place, it is more proper to say that the College of *William and Mary* was in Foundation and Establishment the second College in the Colonies, *Harvard* College in the *Massachusetts Bay* having been founded in 1636, or thereabouts. Yet, it can be said in Truth that the College of *William and Mary* was the first College of royal Foundation in all the *English America*.

❀ ❀ ❀

WHILE the College was yet building at *Middle Plantation*, in the Year 1698, a final Calamity fell upon *Jamestown* in the Burning of the new State House at that Place. And, now, the

[14]

Desire to establish the Seat of Government in a more central and healthful Spot having gained great Strength, and the Plan having found the strong Support of the Governor, the Hon. *Francis Nicholson*, Esq., *Middle Plantation* was brought forward in this Wise:

" . . . and forasmuch as the Place commonly call-
" ed and knowne by the Name of y^e *Middleplanta-*
" *tion* hath been found by const^t Experience to be
" healthy and agreeable to the Constitutions of y^e
" Inhabitants of y^s His Majestyes Colony and Do-
" minion haveing the naturall Advantage of a
" serene and temperate Aire dry and champaign
" Land and plentifully stored with wholesome
" Springs and the Conveniency of two navigable
" and pleas^t Creeks that run out of *James* and *York*
" Rivers necessary for the Supplying the Place with
" Provisions and other Things of Necessity . . . "

So that the Thought of rebuilding the State House at *Jamestown* could not stand in the Face of so handsome a Reputation; and in the Year 1699 the Assembly was prevailed upon to pass an Act entitled *An Act directing the Building the Capitoll and the City of Williamsburgh*, which, among other Things in its great Length, directed that the City to be built at *Middle Plantation* " in Honour " of our most gratious & glorious King *William*, " shall be for ever hereafter called and known by " the Name of the City of *Williamsburgh*."

THIS, then, is the Story of *Williamsburg*, and how, under the Name of *Middle Plantation*, it came about and grew through the seventeenth

Century of our Lord's Time. And, in *Virginia*, this had been a brave and arduous Span; a Time of Massacres and Wars, of Plagues and hard Living; a Time of little Lace and less fine Dancing; a frugal Time in which free Men, with their white indentured Servants (for there were then few Blacks), and even Gentlemen laboured with the Strength and Sweat of their Bodies to gain a Hold in a savage and virgin Wilderness. And, further, it was a Time in which *English* Men reached out for Land, Land for themselves and a Dominion for their King; so that the People were scattered Abroad, and there were few Towns. But now the first Fruits of these Labours were won; and so, as *Virginia* stood before the Spread of another Century, *Williamsburg* rose up—a Metropolis in the new World.

A BRIEF & TRUE REPORT
CONCERNING
WILLIAMSBURG
in VIRGINIA

CHAPTER II.

I T has been held that the History of the chief City of a Country is, in great Measure, the History of that Country itself. And if there be any Truth in this Philosophy, it will be left to the Reader to judge how much greater would be that Truth if the chief City should also be the only City of Consequence in such a Country: For, through those Years of the eighteenth Century in which it was the Metropolis of the *Virginia* Colony, *Williamsburg* was not only the Seat of *Virginia's* Government, but also the principal Seat of its Religion, Education, Society, Commerce, and Fashion. Moreover, it enjoyed this unusual Distinction in a Colony which was then everywhere acknowledged to be the most populous, the most powerful, and the most prosperous of all *Great Britain's* Plantations in *America*; so that though *Williamsburg* was in *Virginia* what *Boston* was in *Massachusetts* and what *Philadelphia* was in *Pennsylvania*, yet, because of its unusual Importance in *Virginia* and because of *Virginia's* Ascendancy among the Colonies, it was (although smaller in Size) in many Ways more potent than even those great Places.

FROM this the Reader will plainly see that it were as simple to pour the *Chesapeake* Bay into a Thimble or to thrust the Tower of *London* into a Snuffbox, as to press the full History of *Williamsburg* between these Covers. Yet, in an opposite Case, it is not surprising that many find it most curious, the History of the City being so broad and imposing, that they have not heard more of it from their Schools and Histories in the Past. And, as to this, it should be made clear that the History of the Colony and of this Capital City were so closely bound together that Historians for these Years needed but to write either a History of *Williamsburg*, or a History of *Virginia*; and so chose the latter. And, having made this Choice, they so long assumed that the true Importance of *Williamsburg* would be remembered, that they have some of them forgot it themselves.

MOREOVER, it should be well noted that *Williamsburg* has ever been a Place of great Extremes—one which, taken from one View or another, was both great and small, both rich and poor, both populous and deserted, both magnificent and wretched, depending upon the Mind that looked upon it and the Rule by which it was tested. And this will be fully shown.

※ ※ ※

THE Act directing the Building of the Capitol and the City of *Williamsburg* at *Middle Plantation*, which was passed by the Assembly (with the Urging of his Excellency, *Francis Nicholson*, Esq., the Governor) in *June*, 1699, set aside two Hundred eighty-three Acres, thirty-five Poles and a Half of Land for the sole Use of the City to be there built. Of this, two Hundred and twenty Acres were surveyed and allotted to the City proper, and the Rest was set aside for two Ports to be known as *Queen Mary's* Port and *Princess Anne* Port (together with Land for Roads leading to them) upon *Queen's* Creek and *Archer's Hope* or *Princess* Creek, so that the City's Bounds might be accessible from the *James* and *York* Rivers, yet the City proper not subject to Bombardment from either.

AND the Portion of *Middle Plantation* thus set aside was, despite its fine History in the Past, a sorry Place at best; it bordering upon the College Lands and containing a Church (which was in poor Condition), a Magazine (which was probably in worse), a few Stores, Mills and inhabited Dwellings, and (it is likely) a Publick House or so—all of which had for a Street an old Horseway.

[19]

Yet, this was of small Concern to the Governor and the Assembly, and, if anything, it was an Assistance to their Purpose; for it was now deliberately intended to raise a new and well ordered City according to a careful and prepared Design, suitable for the Reception of a considerable Number and Concourse of People.

O N E Historian of the Times has said that the Governor proposed to lay out the new City in the form of a Cipher composed of a *W* and an *M*, and others have said that he proposed but a *W*; and it matters little which had the Truth of it, for the Proposal, whatever it was, was abandoned, and the City was laid out upon a principal Street which ran near a Mile on a Straight, and which, in Honour of his Highness *William*, Duke of *Gloucester*, was called the *Duke of Gloucester* Street. And two parallel Streets, one on either Side of the principal Street, were run and were called *Francis* and *Nicholson* Streets in Honour of the Governor; besides which numerous other Streets were run at various Times and were named for the Kingdoms of *Great Britain* and in Honour of royal or publick Persons. And most of these Streets survive to this present Day, together with their Names; among which are *England, Ireland*, and *Scotland* Streets, *King* and *Queen* Streets, *Prince George*, *Henry, Nassau*, and *Botetourt* Streets, and many others.

I T is likely that, for some Space at least, the *Duke of Gloucester* Street followed the old Horse-

way, but not for its whole Length; for it was necessary to dismantle four old Houses and an Oven belonging to Mr. *John Page* (from whom much of
the Land for the Building of the City had been
purchased) which stood in the Middle of the
Street at one Point. And the Street was set so that
the College, which had been completed, stood at
its western End; and now the Assembly set aside a
four Hundred seventy-five Foot Square of Land at
its eastern End for a Building to be known by the
Name of the *Capitol*, the Act giving the most
minute and thoughtful Description of how it was
to be built and adorned.

THE first Act, together with supplemental Acts,
for building the Capitol and the City appear in
the Appendix of the third and fully annotated
Edition of this Work, but it should be mentioned
here that, in addition to many of the foregoing
Instructions, they contain, besides others, the fol-
lowing Provisions: That his Excellency *Francis
Nicholson*, Esq., his Majesty's Lieutenant and
Governor General of *Virginia*; *Edmund Jenings*,
Esq., of his Majesty's honourable Council; *Philip
Ludwell*, Esq., and *Thomas Ballard*, Gentleman,
Members of the right worshipful House of Bur-
gesses; *Lewis Burwell*, *Philip Ludwell*, Jr., *John
Page*, *Henry Tyler*, *James Whaley*, and *Benjamin
Harrison*, Jr., Gentlemen, be appointed the Direc-
tors for the Settlement and Encouragement of the
City; that the City be laid out and proportioned
into half Acre Lots, and that the whole Country

have timely Notice of the Act, and an equal Liberty in the Choice of Lots; that no Person should build upon the *Duke of Gloucester* Street a House of less than ten Foot Pitch, and that Houses upon this Street should come within six Feet of the Street and should front alike; that the Building (within twenty-four Months' Time) of a House of stated Size or greater, depending upon the Location, be required for the Reserving of Lots and to prevent their escheating to the Trustees for the City's Lands; that Persons having Lots contiguous to the great Street should enclose the said Lots with a Wall, Pales, or Post and Rails, within six Months after the Building (which the Law required) should be finished. And the whole Act was directed to the Building and Ordering of a City suitable for the Accommodation and Entertainment of the considerable Number of Persons that must, of Necessity, resort thither; so that it was held that the City would probably prove highly advantageous and beneficial to the Success of his Majesty's royal College of *William and Mary*.

AND it was a fortunate Condition that the College Building was standing when the Government came to *Williamsburg*, for, while the Capitol was raising at the opposite End of the Street, the Offices of the Government and the Assemblies were seated there from 1700 to the Year 1704. Besides which, in these Years his Excellency, Governor *Nicholson*, had his own Offices in the

College for some Time, which lent no small Distinction to the new Institution. Yet, it is to be questioned whether his Excellency's Influence upon the Scholars was of the best; for, on one Occasion at the least, being approached in the Halls of the College by one seeking Money out of the publick Funds, the Governor did fly into such a Rage and did curse and swear so loudly, that a Sea Captain, who lay asleep at some Distance in the Building, sprang from his Bed and, neglecting to affix his wooden Leg, came leaping through the Halls in his Shirt, thinking the Building to be afire again, as it often was.

YET, it would be presumptuous to assume that it was because of such Things that his Excellency *Edward Nott*, Esq., who succeeded *Nicholson* as Governor in the Year 1705, was able in 1706 to secure from the Assembly the Passage of an Act directing the Building of a House for the Governor, such an Act having been before this constantly refused by the Assembly.

THIS, then, is the Manner in which *Williamsburg* commenced to be built, and grew more in six Years than, as *Middle Plantation*, it had grown in sixty-six. And it is a Credit to the Reputations of those who had a Hand in these Affairs that the Plan for a City which they arrived at has not required altering and meddling in for these two Hundred Years and more.

IN the Year 1710 Colonel *Alexander Spotswood*, a Man of great Vigour and many Abilities, came out to *Virginia* as the Lieutenant-Governor and as the Successor to *Edmund Jenings*, the President of the Council, who had served as acting Governor for four Years, since the Death of Governor *Nott* in 1706, (*Robert Hunter*, who had been commissioned to succeed *Nott*, having been captured on his Way to *America*). And *Spotswood* found the Capitol in its full Grandeur, it having been first used by the Assembly in 1704, and finally completed in the Year 1705. The Governor's House he found well advanced, but the Work at a Halt, so that he set himself to bring it to Completion; which Aim he pursued with such Zeal and Aspiration that in 1718 he was charged by the Burgesses with lavishing away the Country's Funds. And it is of Interest to note that, as one Appropriation followed upon another, the Building came to be known as the *Palace* for the Governor, instead of as the Governor's House, which was intended at the first; and the Name *Palace* has continued for it.

THE College, to the Sorrow of the Country, *Spotswood* found in Ruin, it having been damaged by a Fire in 1705; but now (in the Words of one of the Times) it was rebuilt, and nicely contrived, altered and adorned by the ingenious Direction of the Governor. Moreover, the brick Church which had been built at *Middle Plantation* in 1683 being

[24]

now in ruinous Condition, and the Vestry having been for some Time desirous of rebuilding it, Governor *Spotswood* encouraged this Design also. On Behalf of the Assembly, he presented a Draught or Plan for the Enlargement of the Church proposed by the Vestry, and offered a generous Subscription to it; and this Church, which yet stands, was in those Days described as being a large, strong Piece of Brickwork in the Form of a Cross, nicely regular and convenient, and adorned as the best Churches in *London*. And it would appear that the Governor, through these Things, gained a splendid Reputation for Knowledge in the Design and Advancement of fine Buildings; for in the Year 1714 the Assembly ordered that he be impowered and desired to order and direct the Building of a brick Magazine for the Arms and Ammunition of the Country, at such a Place as he might think proper; and this resulted in a handsome octagonal Structure conveniently placed in the *Market Square* (which was Midway of the great Street), where it still stands. About the same Time, the County Seat of *James City* County being moved from *Jamestown* to *Williamsburg*, a new Court House was built upon the Border of the Market Square and near the Magazine. Meanwhile, many private Dwellings and Publick Houses were raised, and the Streets, especially the great Street, were much improved and levelled. Besides which, about the Year 1716, one *William Levingston* erected a Playhouse or Theatre upon the Avenue near to the Palace, which was the first Theatre to be built in the *English American* Colonies.

N O R were the Energies of Governor *Spotswood* directed solely to the Upbuilding of the City of *Williamsburg*; for in his Time there was a steady Increase of Prosperity in the Colony, to which the Governor endeavored to add by the Encouragement of various Manufactures. And Piracy upon the Seas, which was a Hinderance to Prosperity, he sought to put down by an Expedition which he sent out against one *Edward Teach*, who was better known as *Blackbeard*; and this Expedition returned with *Blackbeard's* Head swung upon a Bowsprit and with certain of his Followers in Irons, who were later tried at *Williamsburg* and afterwards hanged. Moreover, the *French* and their *Indians* having commenced to be a Menace in the western Lands, *Spotswood*, in the Year 1716, led a Company of about fifty Gentlemen (who have since been called the *Knights of the Golden Horseshoe*) in a great exploratory March to the Mountains of the *Blue Ridge*, upon a Peak of which they drank King *George's* Health in a brave Assortment of Wines and Spirits; and, to assure that the Land was fairly taken, they proceeded into the fertile Plains in the Valley of the *Shenandoah* beyond, where they planted a Claim in an emptied Bottle. And it would appear that the Governor's Purpose was to extend and settle the

Virginia Colony to the westward, so that it might become a Barrier to the *French* Line of Communication between Lake *Erie* and *Louisiana*.

IN the Year 1717 an Endeavour was made under a previous Act of Parliament to settle the *British* Postal System in *Virginia* (as it had already been settled in some of the northern Colonies) by the Establishment of a Post to run each Fortnight between *Williamsburg* and *Philadelphia*. And it is of Interest to note that the *Virginians* immediately and loudly protested that Parliament could levy no Tax (for they considered the Rates of Postage to be such) without the Consent of their General Assembly (and, as to this, it should be explained that the Assembly itself, almost from its first Beginning in 1619, had claimed the sole Right to tax *Virginians*). Now, in 1718, Laws were passed by the Assembly which would have defeated the new Postal System, had not the Governor refused his Assent to them. Thus, *Virginia* early exhibited a Distaste for Stamp Taxes, which, as will be shown, was not a passing Prejudice. And the Dislike in which the new System was held at *Williamsburg* is shown by a Letter written in 1718 by Col. *John Custis*, the Father of the first Husband of Mrs. *Martha Dandridge Custis Washington*, which went as follows:

"Wee have a damn'd confounded, pretended "Post Office here, wch keeps Letters as long as they "think fitt; it is a generall Grievance to y^e "Country: but am not sure of its being redressed.

" I desire you to putt all my Letters in a small Box;
" directed to me, and give y^m into ye Capt^s Charge;
" and then I may bee in some Hopes of having y^m
" safe and not peep'd into; a Form of Land Piracy
" to practicable in *Virg^a* nowadays . . . "

WITHIN the next few Years *Spotswood* entered upon several Disagreements with the Assembly, besides which he fell at Odds about the Clergy with the Reverend Dr. *Blair*, the President of the College and Commissary of the Bishop of *London*, who has been pointed to by Historians as the Rock upon which Governors *Andros* and *Nicholson* had already foundered; so that in 1722 he was relieved of his Commission as Lieutenant-Governor. Yet, *Spotswood* continued to live in the Colony, and, though his Years as Governor were not unscarred by some Dispute and Contention, yet was he generally held in high Esteem and considered a Friend to *Virginia*. Moreover, when, in the Year 1724, the Reverend *Hugh Jones* prepared and published in *England* his History called *The Present State of Virginia*, he wrote:

"Though they [the *Virginians*] are permitted to
" trade to no Parts but *Great Britain* . . . yet
" have they in many Respects better and cheaper
" Commodities than we in *England*, especially of
" late Years; for the Country may be said to be
" altered and improved in Wealth and polite Liv-
" ing within these few Years, since the Beginning of
" Col. *Spotswood's* Government, more than in all
" the Scores of Years before that, from its first
" Discovery."

Moreover, this same and reverend Author, who was for some Years before his Return to *England* a Citizen of *Williamsburg* (he having been Professor of Mathematicks at the College and the Chaplain to the House of Burgesses), wrote also in his Work a full Description of the publick Buildings in *Williamsburg*, saying that they were justly reputed the best in all the *English America* and exceeded by few of their Kind in *England*. The College and the Capitol he described at great Length, the latter being styled the best and most commodious Pile of its Kind that he had seen or heard of. The Palace he disposed of in briefer Space and in the following Manner:

" From the Church runs a Street northward
" called *Palace* Street; at the other End of which
" stands the Palace or Governor's House, a mag-
" nificent Structure, built at the publick Expence,
" finished and beautified with Gates, fine Gardens,
" Offices, Walks, a fine Canal, Orchards, &c. . . .
" This likewise has the ornamental Addition of a
" good Cupola or Lanthorn, illuminated with most
" of the Town, upon Birth-Nights, and other
" Nights of occasional Rejoicings.

" At the Capitol, at Publick Times, may be seen
" a great Number of handsom, well-dress'd, com-
" pleat Gentlemen. And at the Governor's House
" upon Birth-Nights, and at Balls and Assemblies,
" I have seen as fine an Appearance, as good Diver-
" sion, and as splendid Entertainments in Governor
" *Spotswood's* Time, as I have seen any where
" else."

And the Capital City itself this same Author described in this Fashion:

"*Williamsburgh* is now incorporated and made a "Market Town, and governed by a Mayor and "Aldermen; and is well stock'd with rich Stores, of "all Sorts of Goods, and well furnished with the "best Provisions and Liquors.

"Here dwell several very good Families, and "more reside here in their own Houses at Publick "Times.

"They live in the same neat Manner, dress after "the same Modes, and behave themselves exactly "as the Gentry in *London;* most Families of any "Note having a Coach, Chariot, Berlin, or Chaise.

"The Number of Artificers is here daily aug-"mented; as are the convenient Ordinaries or Inns "for Accommodation of Strangers.

"The Servants here, as in other Parts of the "Country, are *English, Scotch, Irish,* or *Negroes.*

"The Town is laid out regularly in Lots or square "Portions, sufficient each for a House and Garden; "so that they don't build contiguous, whereby may "be prevented the spreading Danger of Fire; and "this also affords a free Passage for the Air, which "is very grateful in violent hot Weather.

"Here, as in other Parts, they build with Brick, "but most commonly with Timber lined with Ciel-"ing, and cased with feather-edged Plank, painted "with white Lead and Oil, covered with Shingles "of Cedar, &c. tarr'd over at first; with a Passage "generally through the Middle of the House for "an Air-Draught in Summer.

"Thus their Houses are lasting, dry, and warm "in Winter, and cool in Summer; especially if there "be Windows enough to draw the Air.

" Thus they dwell comfortably, genteely, pleas-
" antly, and plentifully in this delightful, health-
" ful, and (I hope) thriving City of *Williams-*
" *burgh.*"

And the Reverend Mr. *Jones* prayed that the College in *Williamsburg* might become a laudable
Nursery and a strong Bulwark against the " con-
" tagious Dissentions in *Virginia,*" which Colony,
in the most glowing Terms, he described in this
Wise:

" . . . the most antient and loyal, the most plen-
" tiful and flourishing, the most extensive and bene-
" ficial Colony belonging to the Crown of *Great*
" *Britain,* upon which it is most directly dependant;
" . . .
" Most other Plantations, especially they that
" are granted away to Proprietors, are inferior to
" *Virginia:* . . . whereas *Virginia* is esteemed
" one of the most valuable Gems in the Crown of
" *Great Britain.* . . .
" If *New England* be called a Receptacle of Dis-
" senters, and an *Amsterdam* of Religion, *Pensyl-*
" *vania* the Nursery of *Quakers, Maryland* the
" Retirement of *Roman Catholicks, North Carolina*
" the Refuge of Run-aways, and *South Carolina*
" the Delight of Buccaneers and Pyrates, *Virginia*
" may be justly esteemed the happy Retreat of true
" *Britons* and true Churchmen for the most Part;
" neither soaring too high nor drooping too low,
" consequently should merit the greater Esteem
" and Encouragement."

AND these Things written by a Man of the
Cloth and one given to the Accuracies of Mathematicks, who had dwelt in the Colony, yet was

distant from it at the Time of his Writing, should be of Interest to the Reader; for it will be seen from them that *Virginia* had now suddenly left the Coarseness of its pioneer Times, and had commenced to display the Polish of full Establishment. And whether *Williamsburg* was the Reason of this new Era or the first Result of it, would be difficult to say; but there can be no Question that it was now in full Truth the chief City of the Colony. ❀ ❀ ❀

COLONEL *Spotswood* was succeeded as the Lieutenant-Governor by the Honourable *Hugh Drysdale* in 1722; and, upon *Drysdale's* dying in 1726, Colonel *Robert Carter*, the President of the Council, served as Governor for about a Year's Time, until the Year 1727, in which the Honourable *William Gooch*, Esq., came out to *Virginia* as the Lieutenant-Governor.

THE twenty-two Years of Governor *Gooch's* Administration have ever been known as a Time of great Prosperity and Advancement in *Virginia*; for that Gentleman was possessed of the scarce and happy Capacity to balance the Assembly on the one Hand against the Lords of Trade upon the other, and to smile with Amiableness upon the People besides. So that the Laws, especially those that controlled the Trade in Tobacco, were vastly improved, to the Advantage of the Planters. The Revenues were better regulated and increased, to the Pleasure of the Lords of Trade; and the

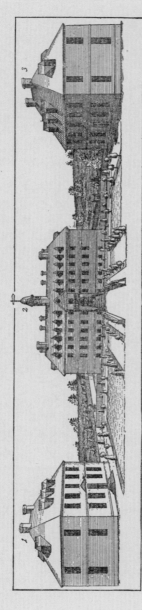

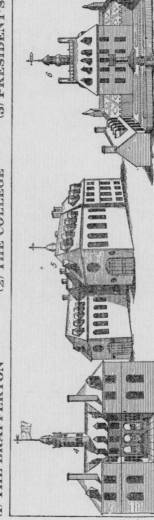

(1) THE BRAFFERTON   (2) THE COLLEGE   (3) PRESIDENT'S HOUSE

(4) THE CAPITOL   (5) THE COLLEGE (REAR)   (6) THE PALACE

*From an Engraving made in the Year 1740, or thereabout, the Original of which was presented by the Bodleian Libraries,
Oxford, to Mr. John D. Rockefeller, Jr., in 1937.*

Colony was extended and settled to the westward, to the Benefit of the whole Country and to the Glory of the Crown. Thus, whereas *Spotswood* had built Prosperity, *Gooch* built yet greater Prosperity upon it.

AND this Prosperousness in the Country was reflected upon its Capital City in the Growth and Importance of that Place, and, in a Sense, it was reflected back to the Country again; for the Influence of the fine Design, Character, and Craftsmanship displayed in the prominent early Buildings of *Williamsburg* was (and yet is) to be seen in many of the great Plantation Houses which commenced to be raised on Gentlemen's Estates about this Time.

AND it may be taken that the Understanding between the Government and the People was, in some Measure, increased by the Arrival in *Williamsburg* of *William Parks*, one of the foremost Printers of those Times; who opened an Office in the City about 1730 and, in the Year 1736, commenced to print the *Virginia Gazette*, which was the first Newspaper in *Virginia*, and one of the earliest in the Colonies. Moreover, about 1744, *Parks*, with the friendly Assistance of *Benjamin Franklin*, of *Philadelphia*, began the Manufacture of Paper in a Mill which he erected on the Outskirts of the City, and which he advanced as " the " first Mill of the Kind, that ever was erected in " this Colony. "

THOSE who deal in Matters of History have commonly found Times of Tranquillity and Success to be ill-suited to their Business; and so it is that those quiet Years of Governor *Gooch's* Government may herein be given over to a Discussion of the true Nature of the City of *Williamsburg*, which, for the Understanding of the Reader, should now be explained:

A T the first it should be made plain that, though it became a City Incorporate in the Year 1722, *Williamsburg*, in the Time of Governor *Gooch,* numbered not more than one Thousand resident Persons (both white and black), nor more than two Hundred Houses. Moreover, it should be stated that at no Time in its History as the Capital of *Virginia* did it number greatly more than two Thousand resident Persons, nor more than three Hundred Houses. Yet, the Reader should be mindful of the Fact that these Figures represented in that Time a proportionate Part of the Population of the Colony as great as that represented by many Capital Cities in our present Day. Besides which, it should also be held in Mind that the great Wealth of *Virginia* in those Years sprang from Tobacco, and Tobacco sprang from the Land; so that even a Thousand Persons gathered together in a City was a rare Thing indeed. Thus it was that Lord *Adam Gordon*, who visited *Virginia* in 1764, wrote in his Journal the following:

" They live at their own Seats and are seldom at
" *Williamsburg* but when the publick Business re-

"quires their Attendance, or that their own pri-
"vate Affairs call them there, scarce any of the
"topping People have Houses there of their own,
"but in the Country they live on their Estates
"handsomely and plentifully, raising all they
"require and depending for Nothing on the
"Market."

YET, if limited in Numbers, the resident Citizens of *Williamsburg* composed an active and di-
verse Population; for, at one Time and another,
besides the Officials of the Government and the
College, they included among them:

Actors
Apothecaries
Attorneys
Bakers
Barbers &
    Hairdressers
Blacksmiths &
    Farriers
Bricklayers &
    Masons
Butchers
Cabinet Makers
Carpenters
Chandlers &
    Soap-boilers
Clerks
Coach & Riding
    Chairmakers
Coopers
Coppersmiths
Cutlers
Dancing Masters

Doctors
Gardeners
Glaziers
Goldsmiths &
Gunsmiths
    Silversmiths
Hatters
Jailers
Jewelers
Joiners
Lead Workers
Mantua-Makers
Merchants
Midwives
Millers
Milliners
Ministers
Musicians
Plaisterers
Post Riders
Potash Makers
Printers

Sadlers &
    Harnessmakers
Sawyers
Servants
Shipwrights &
    Shipmasters
Shoemakers
Snuffmakers
Staymakers
Surgeon-
    Dentists
Surveyors
Tailors
Tanners
Tavern Keepers
Tinsmiths
Watchmakers
Weavers
Wheelwrights
Wigmakers &
    Perukers
&c. &c. &c.

[35]

BUT it should be marked that it was not in normal Seasons of the Year, when Men went about their usual daily Tasks and the City was concerned only with its casual Offices as Capital and County Seat, that *Williamsburg* enjoyed its true Prominence and Power. It was during the Publick Times (usually in the *Spring* and *Fall*) when the Assemblies were held or the Courts sat "with a "Dignity and Decorum that would become them "even in *Europe*" that the City became the true Metropolis: For then the Population was increased from one and two Thousand Persons to five and six Thousand; then the Taverns, Inns, Publick Houses, Ordinaries, private Dwellings, and nearby Plantations were filled to overflowing; then all Men of publick Office or Prominence, and even most Persons of private Wealth or Consequence thronged to *Williamsburg*, as did those who lived by their Wits and the Influence to be sought there. So that there was no publick Commotion to be seen in all *Virginia*, or elsewhere in the Colonies, which would compare with *Williamsburg* at Publick Times; for as *Virginians* lived apart, so they came together, and the Isolation of a Half-year was lost in a Fortnight or more of Society, Merriment, Commerce, and Politicks, so long as the Assembly stood convened.

AND of such great Moment were these Publick Times, that most Events that could be so adjusted were set to fall within them: So that the Fairs, which were held in *April* and *December*, often coincided with such Occasions, lending a Side-play of Puppet Shows, Contests in Beauty, Fiddling, Dancing, Foot Races from the College to the Capitol, Cudgellings, and Chases for Pigs to be caught by the Tails (which were soaped). Moreover, the Season in the Theatre reached its Height at such Times; Race Meetings for the best Horses were held upon the Mile Course near the City, and, doubtless, Matches between the prize Cocks of different Sections were fought; the Craftsmen then displayed their finest Works, and the Merchants advanced the latest Fashions out of *London*; Slave Auctions were held; the Prize-winners in Lotteries and Raffles were announced; and the Merchants and Men of Affairs gathered upon *The Exchange* beyond the Capitol, where Debts were paid and contracted and the Money Business of the Country transacted.

T H E best People of every Section of the Colony stopped in *Williamsburg* and appeared in its Streets at Publick Times; so that even an ill-disposed Traveller out of *England*, who could find Nothing considerable in *Williamsburg* save the Capitol, the Palace, and the College (which he admitted to be "no bad Piles"), wrote of his Amazement at "the prodigious Number of "Coaches that croud the deep sandy Streets of "this little City." These were the People who were in Attendance at the elegant Balls, Banquets, Lawn Fetes, and Displays of Fireworks given at the Palace; so that Colonel *Spotswood* showed

small Concern in reporting that upon an official
Occasion he had entertained two Hundred Guests
at his House, and Governor *Gooch* was later able
to state in a Letter to his Brother " The Gentm.
" and Ladies here are perfectly well bred, not an
" ill Dancer in my Govmt. " And the Popularity
of the City with the fine People is further shown
by Letters such as the following, which would
seem to have been written by a forlorn Suitor:

" . . . I flatter'd myself with the Pleasure of see-
" ing Miss *Bassett* in *Hanover* before this Time,
" but I suppose she intends staying below, to par-
" take of the Mirth of the Metropolis, and come
" to *Han*ʳ. to take a Respite from Dancing, as she
" knows this is no Place for Jollity . . . "

NOR is it remarkable, in the Light of these
Things, that an unusual Number of Taverns and
Publick Houses sprang up in *Williamsburg*; of
which Number the *Raleigh* Tavern (which was
built sometime before 1742) stood forth as the
foremost Hostelry for the fine People, and as a
social gathering Place second only to the Palace
itself.

YET, it should be stated that Celebrations in
Williamsburg were not entirely confined to Publick Times; for even when the Assembly was not
convened, nor the Courts in Session, such Reports
as the following appeared in the *Virginia Gazette:*

" Last *Friday* being the Anniversary of our most
" gracious Sovereign's Accession to the Throne, his
" Excellency the Governour gave a Ball and an
" elegant Entertainment at the Palace, to a numer-

" ous and splendid Company of Ladies and Gentle-
" men. The *Raleigh* Tavern likewise, by Direction
" of his Excellency, was opened for the Entertain-
" ment of Such as might incline to spend the Even-
" ing there; plenty of Liquor was given to the Pop-
" ulace; and the City was handsomely illuminated."

SUCH, then, was the true and twofold Nature
of *Williamsburg* when it was the Seat of Government; and if one Chronicler described it as re-
sembling a small Country Town in *England*, and
another saw it as a boiling Metropolis in the new
World, they both had some Truth upon their
Sides, depending upon when they came thither.

AND if the Reader should harbour Doubts in his
Mind concerning these Things, he may find for
himself in the Records not less, but more.

❖ ❖ ❖

NO Treatise upon the true Nature of the City
of *Williamsburg* could be considered complete that lacked some Discussion of the College of
William and Mary in *Virginia*, for that Institution has ever been a great Ornament to the City
and an Honour to the whole Country. And as the
Virginia Colony and the City of *Williamsburg* are
bound together in History, so are the City and its
College bound; and an Endeavor to treat the one
without the other would result in a Distortion.

AT its first Foundation the College, in Accord-
ance with the Supplication of the Assembly, was
designed to the End that the Church of *Virginia*
might be furnished with a Seminary of Ministers

of the Gospel, that the Youth might be piously educated in good Letters and Manners, and the *Christian* Faith might be propagated amongst the Western *Indians*, to the Glory of *Almighty God*. And the Charter of the College, which was granted in the Year 1693, looked toward a perpetual College for Divinity, Philosophy, Languages, and other fine Arts and Sciences, consisting of one President, six Masters or Professors, and a Hundred Scholars, more or less, Graduates and Non-Graduates.

WITH these worthy Objects in view, the College grew but slowly at the first (as most Things of great Worth should) ; it beginning with a Grammar School, in which were taught *Latin* and *Greek*, and a common School in which *Indians* were taught "Reading, Writing, and vulgar "Arithmatick." And, though a Professorship of Natural Philosophy and Mathematicks was added by 1711, the Curriculum was not much advanced beyond this for some Time; so that the Reverend Mr. *Hugh Jones* was justified in writing the following in his History as late as 1724:

"As for Education several are sent to *England*
"for it; though the *Virginians* being naturally of
"good Parts, (as I have already hinted) neither
"require nor admire as much Learning, as we do in
"*Britain;* yet more would be sent over, were they
"not afraid of the Small-Pox, which most common-
"ly proves fatal to them.
"But indeed when they come to *England* they
"are generally put to learn to Persons that know

" little of their Temper, . . .

" For Grammar Learning taught after the com-
" mon round-about Way is not much beneficial nor
" delightful to them; so that they are noted to be
" more apt to spoil their School-Fellows than im-
" prove themselves; . . .

" Thus the Youth might as well be instructed
" there as here by proper Methods, without the
" Expence and Danger of coming hither; especially
" if they make Use of the great Advantage of the
" College at *Williamsburgh*, . . . "

AND it would appear that the *Virginians* soon
thereafter began to recognize the Advantage of
their College; for by the Year 1729 its Faculty had
reached the full Complement specified in its Charter, and included, besides the President, a Professor of Natural Philosophy and Mathematicks, a
Professor of Moral Philosophy, two Professors of
Divinity, the Master of the Grammar School, the
Master of the *Indian* School, and an Usher.
Moreover, the *Indian* School was now established
in a new Building to itself called the *Brafferton*,
which had been built in the Year 1723; opposite
to which, upon the College Grounds, a handsome
House for the President was built in the Year
1732. And these two Structures, together with the
great College Building, stand to this present Day.

BY the Year 1754 there were sixty-seven Scholars and Students boarded at the College, besides
eight *Indians*; and it has been conjectured that
about forty other Students resided or boarded in
the City. So that there were in all about one Hun-

dred and fifteen in Attendance. And though this
Number did not greatly increase, the Scheme of
the College was changed from Time to Time as
the Years advanced, the Grammar School and the
Indian School being discontinued, and new advanced Schools or Professorships being added.
And in this Process the College accumulated an
Assortment of Priorities in *American* Education,
a Listing of which would weary the Reader with
its Length and Detail.

A N D it should be pointed to that if the College
was a great Adornment to the Reputation and Life
of *Williamsburg*, the City, by Way of Return, provided the College with an unsurpassed and ready
Laboratory of Society, Politicks, and Government.
Thus, if the College gave to *Virginia* a Majority
of those who shaped its Destinies in its Progress
from a loyal Colony to a Leader of Rebellion,
and so to a free and independent State, it should
be remembered that *Williamsburg* had already
schooled these Leaders in the Ways of good Government and polite Living before they came to the
Halls of its Capitol. As a single Example of this
Truth may be advanced the Autobiography of
Thomas Jefferson, who wrote of Dr. *William
Small* (one of the Professors of the College) as the
man who "fixed the Destinies of my Life" and
who "filled up the Measure of his Goodness to me,
"by procuring for me, from his most intimate
"Friend *G. Wythe*, a Reception as a Student of
"Law, under his Direction, and introduced me to

" the Acquaintance and familiar Table of Govern-
" or *Fauquier*—the ablest Man who ever filled
" that Office. "

A s to the Success of the College in the Field of
Divinity, a late Historian, the good Bishop *William Meade*, bears Witness in this Wise: " The
" best Ministers in *Virginia* were those educated at
" the College and sent over to *England* for Ordi-
" nation. The Foreigners were the great Scandal
" of the Church. "

A n d since the full and true History of the College cannot here be given, it is a happy Circum-
stance that the real Worth of a College may best
be seen in the Accomplishments of its Students:
Thus, it should be of Interest to the Reader to note
that, in addition to that Host of publick Figures
the College gave to the *Virginia* Colony, it gave to
the united Colonies sixteen Members of the Continental Congress at *Philadelphia* (including *Peyton Randolph*, of *Williamsburg*, the first President
of that Body), and to the *Declaration of Independence* it gave four Signatures—those of *George
Wythe*, *Thomas Jefferson*, *Carter Braxton*, and
Benjamin Harrison. To the new Nation brought
about by these Things, the College gave four of
the first ten Presidents—*George Washington*
(who, though not a Student of the College, was
commissioned a Surveyor by the College and who
was afterwards its Chancellor), *Thomas Jefferson,
James Monroe*, and *John Tyler*. Besides which,

[43]

to the Federal Government the College has given four Justices of the Supreme Court (including *John Marshall*, the great Chief Justice); four Secretaries of State; seventeen Senators from *Virginia* and twelve from seven other States; three Speakers of the House of Representatives, and fifty-eight Members of that Body; four Attorneys General, including *Edmund Randolph*, the first Attorney General; a Secretary of War; a Secretary of the Navy; a Postmaster General; a Secretary of the Treasury; a Secretary of the Interior; eighteen Ministers to nine foreign Countries; and a vast Number of lesser Officials. To the individual States the College has given twenty-seven Governors, including eighteen to *Virginia* and nine to seven other States. And the Reader will be spared from more and others.

THUS, though the College did not fulfill the Hope of the Reverend *Hugh Jones* and become a "strong Bulwark against the contagious Dissen-"tions in *Virginia*," still it would seem to have become as strong in an opposite Cause; so that the Reverend Author and Mathematician did not miscalculate in Strength, but in Direction.

❋ ❋ ❋

TO return to the Sequence of our Narration, it should be stated that upon the Departure of Sir *William Gooch* in the Year 1749 (he resigning because of his Health), the Office of Governor was filled for about three Years by *John Robinson*, *Thomas Lee*, and *Lewis Burwell*, who succeeded in due Order as Presidents of the Council.

I N their Time was commenced the Rebuilding of the Capitol, it having been mysteriously burned in the Year 1747. Moreover, the Palace having fallen into a somewhat ruinous Condition, and it being unoccupied, Work was commenced to repair, enlarge, and adorn that Structure even in Advance of its former Magnificence. Also, in this Time, there came a great Revival of Interest in the Theatre and, *Levingston's* old Playhouse near the Palace having sometime before been given over to the City for a Town Hall, a new Theatre was built beyond and near the Capitol by publick Subscription.

A N D it should be stated here that the Rebuilding of the Capitol at *Williamsburg* was not undertaken without considerable Discussion, Debate, and Ill-feeling in the Assembly. There had been, in Governor *Gooch's* Time, a great Expansion of the Colony to the westward, this coming about both by natural Growth and by a great Influx of *Scotch-Irish Presbyterians* and of *Pennsylvania Germans* into the western Frontier. Thus, when the Capitol burned, a Majority of the Burgesses favored a Removal of the Seat of Government to a more central Spot, and a Place more suitable for direct Navigation. But, Governor *Gooch*, the Council and certain prominent Citizens of the City having come to the Defense of *Williamsburg*, and they being aided by the Fact that the City was singularly free from an Epidemic of *Small-Pox* which was raging in the Colony at that Time, their Motion was carried and *Williamsburg* continued as the Capital.　❀ ❀ ❀

THE Honourable *Robert Dinwiddie*, Esq., arrived in *Williamsburg* to become the Lieutenant-Governor on *November* 21, 1751, and was inducted into Office with a great Ceremony and Celebration, which ended with an elegant Banquet at *Wetherburn's* Tavern. To him the City, through its Mayor, Recorder, Aldermen, and Common Council, delivered an eloquent Address in which was stated:

" . . . His Majesty, always good and gracious to
" his People, could not more agreeably have re-
" paired the Loss we sustained in our late Governor
" Sir *William Gooch,* than by appointing you who
" are so well acquainted with us, our Laws and
" Constitutions, to be his worthy Successor; and we
" hope that your Administration may be longer,
" and if possible more happy, than his. . . . "

B U T, though he was an able and an industrious Gentleman, *Dinwiddie's* Government was not to be blest as that of Governor *Gooch* had been. Moreover, though other capable royal Deputies were to hold the Governorship, neither were their Times to be so blest. In Governor *Dinwiddie's* Case, almost at the Start, he fell at Odds with the Assembly concerning a Fee for the Issuing of Land Patents (which Fee the Burgesses considered a

Tax); and soon after this Disagreement came the War with the *French* and their *Indians*.

AT his first Coming, the Governor and his Family occupied a Dwelling just south and west of the Palace, which House the Assembly had purchased for his Use until the Alterations and Repairs at the Palace should be completed. Yet, by the Year 1752 he was installed in the Palace; for in *November* of that Year he received the Emperor and Empress of the *Cherokee* Nation there, they having come to the City with their Son and their chief Men to treat of Trade and Friendship.

IN the Year 1753 the *Virginia* Colony (its Bounds under its Charter of 1609 having been reduced by Grants to *Maryland*, the *Carolinas*, and *Pennsylvania*) still encompassed what is now the western Part of *Pennsylvania* and the Territory now represented by the States of *West Virginia, Kentucky, Ohio, Indiana, Illinois, Michigan*, and *Wisconsin*; and *Williamsburg* was the Capital of all this vast Dominion. Thus, when the *French* commenced to establish Settlements upon the *Ohio* River, Governor *Dinwiddie* chose as his Emissary, to warn them against such Encroachments, one *George Washington*, a young Man scarce come of Age, who was well fitted for so arduous a Journey by his Work as a Surveyor in the western Wilds.

(HERE it should be of Interest to the Reader to note that the major Courses of *Washington's* Life were shaped in *Williamsburg:* His active military Career commenced with his being sent out from the Palace as the Envoy of the Governor (he having been for sometime Adjutant-General and a Major in the *Virginia* Militia) and with his being subsequently placed in Command of the *Virginia* Militia against the *French*; all of which, in a round-about Fashion, grew out of the Surveyor's Commission which he had gained from the College of *William and Mary*. His political Career, though it was founded upon his military Fame, was justified and strengthened by some sixteen Years spent as a Member of the House of Burgesses, and as a Delegate for *Virginia* to the Continental Congress. His domestic Life began with his Marriage (in the County of *New Kent*) to the Widow of Mr. *Daniel Parke Custis*, she being a Resident of *Williamsburg* and one of the wealthiest Women in all the Country).

IN the Year 1754, it becoming apparent that the *French* would not comply with his Request that they vacate the *Virginia* Territory in the West, *Dinwiddie* again sent *Washington*, now a Lieutenant-Colonel, with three Hundred *Virginia* Militia to the Aid of a Garrison in that Quarter. And this Expedition, meeting with a Party of *French*, and slaying twelve of them, and taking twenty-one Prisoners, brought about the Opening of a War with *France* which was fought up and down the whole *American* Frontier, in *Canada*, and extended into *Europe* and *Asia*.

AND some Historians have held that the War

with the *French* was, in large Measure, responsible for that great Revolt in the Colonies which followed after it; they claiming that it brought the Colonies for the first Time into concerted Action, that it relieved them from the Fear of Invasion by the *French*, that it taught them the Weakness of *British* Regulars in an unfamiliar Land, and that the Expense of the War brought about the Passage of the *Stamp Act*. Yet, it should not be neglected that, no Matter what came of it, the War in *America* was fought by *Great Britain* in Defense of her Colonies and with the loyal Aid of those Colonies.

THE Responsibilities of the War, together with Disagreements with a determined Assembly and the usual heavy Tasks of his Office, overtaxed the Strength of *Dinwiddie*; so that, while the War was yet raging, he asked to be relieved. He left the Colony in *January*, 1758, carrying with him the high Regard of the People and (the Bounds of *Williamsburg* having been increased in his Time) he carried also a Testimonial of Gratitude from the Authorities of the City.

AFTER his Departure, the Honourable *John Blair*, the President of the Council and Nephew of the deceased President of the College, served for a Time as Governor.

❀ ❀ ❀

IN *June* of the Year 1758 the Honourable *Francis Fauquier*, Esq., whom *Thomas Jefferson* (as has already been noted) described as the ablest Man ever to hold the Office, arrived in *Williamsburg* to be Lieutenant-Governor.

I N his Time the Tide of the War with the *French* turned to the Favour of the *English* and their Colonies; so that in 1763 *Fauquier* was able to notify the Assembly of the "Conclusion of a "most glorious and honourable Peace between his "Majesty and all his Enemies." And by the *Treaty of Paris* concluded at this Time, virtually that entire Part of the Continent of *North America* lying East of the *Mississippi* River was assured to the *English*.

G O V E R N O R *Fauquier* has ever been known to the History of *Virginia* as a Man of liberal and popular Views, and as one of great scientific Interests and gentlemanly Pursuits in Learning. And if his Interest in Science led him too often to investigate the Laws of Chance, and thus to establish a Vogue for the Gaming Table in the Colony, yet were his Sins vastly out-weighted by his Virtues (which is the true Test of any Man).

I T has been established that *Fauquier* was forewarned of the Plan to tax the Colonies after the Close of the War with the *French*, and that he, knowing the Temper of the Colonists, advised strongly against such Taxation. Howbeit, the *Stamp Act* was passed by the House of Commons on *February* 27, 1765; and immediately there arose a Storm of Displeasure in the Colonies. Yet, this Displeasure had no popular Expression until one *Patrick Henry*, a young Lawyer newly risen to Prominence through a Defense against the *Parson's Cause*, offered before the House of Burgesses of *Virginia* a Series of Resolutions against the *Stamp Act*. And these Resolutions, being deemed unwise by the more conservative Members of the House, brought on a bitter Debate, especially with Regard to the fifth Resolution, in which it was protested that the sole Right to tax *Virginians* rested with the *Virginia* Assembly and that any Effort to vest this Right elsewhere had a "mani-"fest Tendency to destroy *British* as well as *Ame-*"*rican* Freedom." And it was in the Course of a Defense of this Resolution that *Henry* cried out, "*Cæsar* had his *Brutus*—*Charles* the First his "*Cromwell*—and *George* the Third—" (here, some say, he was interrupted by Cries of "Treason" from the House; and another Witness has said that he was interrupted by the Speaker's rebuking the House for its Complaisance) "—and "*George* the Third," *Henry* continued, "may "profit by their Example. If this be Treason— "make the most of it!"

T H E fifth Resolution was carried in the House of Burgesses by a single Vote; though Mr. *Peyton Randolph*, the Attorney-General and an eminent though conservative Patriot, expostulated in the Lobby, "By *God*, I would have given five Hun-"dred Guineas for a single Vote." And though, on the following Day, *Henry's* fifth Resolution was ordered to be expunged from the Record,

News of the Resolutions and the Action of the Assembly travelled through *Virginia* and throughout the Colonies. Thus, for those that relate Causes and Results, and for those ingenious Persons who can bring themselves to attribute the Beginning of any War to a single Event, the *American* Revolution was born in the Capitol at *Williamsburg* on *May* 30, 1765.

THESE Things, quite naturally, were far too astonishing to be overlooked by even so liberal a Governor as *Fauquier*; and so the Assembly was at once dissolved. And when one *George Mercer* arrived from *England* as the Chief Distributor of the Stamps, *Fauquier* gave him the Protection of his own Person and Company until Mr. *Mercer* publickly announced that he would not undertake the Distribution of the Stamps without the Consent of the Assembly. Moreover, *Fauquier*, with that Wisdom so characteristic of him, continued to prorogue the Assembly until he was able to proclaim to the People on *June* 9, 1766, an Act of Parliament which repealed the hated *Stamp Act*; whereat there was great Rejoicing and Celebrating in *Williamsburg* and through the whole Country.

AND though *Fauquier* fulfilled his Office as the Deputy of the Crown with the greatest Loyalty and Dignity, yet, the People and the Assembly sensed a most sincere Interest and Sympathy beneath all his Actions. So that there was great Mourning in *Virginia* when the Governor died on

March 3, 1768, and was laid at Rest in the north Aisle of *Bruton* Church; while in the *Virginia Gazette* appeared Verses such as the Following:

" If ever Virtue lost a Friend sincere,
" If ever Sorrow claim'd *Virginia's* Tear,
" If ever Death a noble Conquest made,
" 'Twas when *Fauquier* the Debt of Nature paid."

❀ ❀ ❀

IT does not lie within the Power (or Province) of any brief and true Report to trace the Development and Course of the Revolution, nor even to explain the important Part which *Virginia* had in this complicated Affair; for if it sought to unfold the Truth of these Matters, the Brevity of such a Report would soon depart. Yet, though it must (under these Circumstances) be effected by general instead of by detailed Disclosures, the true Significance of *Williamsburg* in Relation to these Things should be explained herein:

I N short, the first Causes of the Revolution may be found in the irreconcilable Divergence between the growing Demands of *Great Britain* as an Empire and the Determination of the Colonies that their Right of Self-Government be recognized. Thus, Parliament was mindful of the Needs of the Empire in the Passage of the *Stamp Act*; whereas the Colonists, on their Side, advanced the Principle of *No Taxation without Representation*. These Differences brought on a War against what the

Colonists considered to be unjust Taxation, and this Disturbance soon turned into a War for Independence.

IN this Cause the Colonies of *Virginia* and *Massachusetts Bay* were, beyond Question, the Leaders; and though an Effort to distinguish the relative Importance of these two can be considered an invidious Thing, *Virginia* may be held with some Truth to have carried the more Weight, both because of its Size and because of the greater Prestige which it enjoyed in *England* and among the other Colonies. An Indication of this last, by Way of Example, may be seen in the Statement of *John Adams* of *Massachusetts* to the Effect that he, in commenting to *Thomas Jefferson* upon the Propriety of the latter's Authorship of the Declaration of Independence, said, " You are a *Virginian*, and " a *Virginian* ought to appear at the Head of this " Business. "

MOREOVER, it should be pointed to that in seeking to effect her Purpose of Taxation and also to subdue the Opposition to this Purpose, *England*, at the first, sent Troops to *Massachusetts*, but *Virginia* she sought to appease with Diplomacy and Politicks. Thus, it is but natural, as it turned out, that *Massachusetts* was the first to enter the Field with Arms, and that *Virginia* became the leading Force in the Field of Politicks; though it is equally true that *Virginia* and *Massachusetts* entered each into both Fields and were by no Means the sole Occupants of either.

AND these Statements are neither intended nor advanced as a full Discussion of a Cause which was common to all the Colonies. They are set forth merely to indicate the true Importance of the City of *Williamsburg*, which is the Concern of this Report; for if *Virginia* was the most influential political Leader of the Colonies in the Revolution, the Position of *Williamsburg*, the political Center of *Virginia*, must become obvious.

❀ ❀ ❀

UPON the Passing of his Excellency, Governor *Francis Fauquier*, the Honourable *John Blair*, Esq., the President of the Council and a strong Supporter of the popular Cause, again served as the acting Governor of *Virginia*.

IT had so happened that in the closing Years of *Fauquier's* Government, *George* III had repented of what he termed to be the fatal Compliance with the Demands of the Colonies for the Repeal of the *Stamp Act*. Moreover, the Chancellor of the *British* Exchequer is said to have protested, "*Eng-* "*land* is undone, if this Taxation is given up." And so new Tax Duties were levied upon the Colonies; whereupon, just before the Death of *Fauquier*, the House of Representatives of *Massachusetts* answered back with a Petition to the King in which were advanced the Rights of the Colonies.

NOW, in the Time of *John Blair,* Esq., and while the other Colonies waited upon its Action,

Virginia's House of Burgesses forwarded from *Williamsburg* a Communication applauding *Massachusetts'* Attention to *American* Liberty and stating that the Steps that they, the Burgesses, had already taken would assure *Massachusetts* of *Virginia's* "fixed Resolution to concur with the other "Colonies in their Application for Redress."

❀ ❀ ❀

IN the Year 1768 *Great Britain* instituted a new Means to revive the fast failing Loyalty of the *Virginia* Colony: For some sixty-two Years the Governors of *Virginia*, though they had enjoyed the full Powers and Privileges of the Office, had in Title and Perquisites been but Deputies of the full Governors, who resided in *England*. But now the Right Honourable *Norborne Berkeley, Baron de Botetourt*, was made the full Governor and was sent out to *Virginia* to reside there. He bore the Title—*His Majesty's Lieutenant, Governor-General and Commander-in-Chief.*

LORD *Botetourt* arrived in the Month of *October* aboard a Man-of-War of some sixty Guns; and he was met with Ceremonies and Celebrations at *Williamsburg* which, if anything, exceeded the Usual, to be in Keeping with his Station. The Honourable *William Nelson*, Esq., (who, as President of the Council, was later to succeed *Botetourt*) spoke thus of these Occurrences in a Letter to a Friend in *London*:

[56]

" Lord *Botetourt* is arrived among us, with the
" greatest Advantages imaginable: for we had
" Time, before his Coming, to receive the most
" favourable Impressions of his Lordship's amiable
" Character & good Disposition towards the
" Colony. He hath been received & wellcomed in
" a Manner, which gives him great Pleasure, & I
" should send you Copies of the several Addresses
" & his Answers to them, if I were not well assured
" that you will see them in the publick Papers be-
" fore this can reach you. . . . Among them you
" will find that of the Merchants & Traders (*An-*
" *drew Sprowle* Spokeman) wch I think does
" Honour to that Body, from its Plainness, Ele-
" gance and Simplicity, & far out does the studied
" Performance of the P. & Masters of the College;
" and this Observation being made to *Sprowle,* he
" reply'd (Aye, Sir, the Parsons do Nothing well,
" unless they are paid for it). The old Fellow
" wears his own Hair, as white as old *Charles*
" *Hansford's* was, with a Pig Tail to it, but bald as
" the brave Lord *Granby,* and cuts as droll a
" Figure as ever you saw him in a silk Coat & two
" or three Holes in his Stockings, at the same Time
" he is a respectable Appearance, the oldest among
" the Trade, & acquitted himself well. Indeed, my
" dear Friend, I hope we shall be happy under his
" Lordship's Government, . . . unless . . . when he
" opens his Budget to the Assembly in *May* next,
" Something may be required of them, that is too
" hard of Digestion; however, I will not anticipate
" Misfortunes, nor of myself cast a Cloud over the
" pleasing Prospect before us; and let the Worst

" come, that can come, we are I believe determined
" to a Man to behave with Decency, Duty & Re-
" spect; and, our Cause being a good one, these I
" think are the Means (adding some Firmness) to
" succeed; for Liberty I trust is a good Cause, &
" we may say of it as of Truth, *Magna est et*
" *prævalebit,* if we do not spoil it by our own
" Intemperance, Violence & Folly.   Enough of
" Politicks . . . "

FROM the Time of his first Arriving, Governor
Botetourt gained and held the Respect and Affec-
tion of the People by his Graciousness and Sympathy. To the Address of Welcome by the
President of the College he replied:

" The College of *William and Mary* does
" Honour to this great Country, Ages unborn will
" feel its Effect, and upon this you may depend that
" you cannot oblige me more than by marking out
" any Plan by which I may be enabled to contribute
" to its Advancement and Prosperity."

INDEED, the Friendliness between the Governor and the Colonists soon became so pronounced
that even his Actions against the popular Cause
were looked upon as the Results of unavoidable
Demands of Duty, not as Indications of personal
Sentiment. So that there was Bowing and Smil-
ing upon the Streets of *Williamsburg* when his
Lordship rode forth in the handsome Coach of
State which he had brought with him from *England,* and for which he had six splendid white
Horses.

YET though Friendship existed between the Governor and the Assembly, that same Sentiment was by no Means exchanged between the Assembly and Parliament. And, the Trouble surrounding the Revenue Act having reached such Heights that certain popular Leaders in the Colonies were ordered arrested and transported to *England* for Trial, the House of Burgesses of *Virginia* on *May* 16, 1769, passed a strong Series of Resolutions. In these was again protested the Right of that House to levy Taxes for *Virginia*; and the Transporting of Colonists beyond the Sea for Trial was held to be derogatory to the Rights of *British* Subjects. And Copies of these Resolutions were ordered to be transmitted to the other Colonies. At once the Governor dissolved the Assembly, saying, " I have heard of your Resolves, and augur Ill " of their Effect: You have made it my Duty to " dissolve you; and you are dissolved accord- " ingly." Whereupon, the Burgesses, calling themselves " the late Representatives of the " People," at once reconvened at the *Raleigh* Tavern as a Convention, and there drew up Articles of Association in a Non-Importation Agreement.

IN *New England*, where these Grievances and the Pressure of them was the greater, these Things brought about Riots and Upheavals. But in *Virginia* the general Discontent continued beneath the Surface of such peaceful Scenes as the following, which was described by Miss *Anne Blair* of *Williamsburg* in a Letter written to her Sister in *August*, 1769:

"... Mrs. *Dawson's* Family stay'd ye Evening
"with us, and ye Coach was at ye Door to carry
"them Home, by ten o'Clock; but everyone appear-
"ing in great Spirits, it was proposed to set at y^e
"Steps and Sing a few Songs wch was no sooner
"said than done; while thus we were employ'd, a
"Candle or Lanthorn was observed to be coming
"up Street; (except *Polly Clayton* censuring their
"ill Taste, for having a Candle such a fine Night)
"no one took any Notice of it—till we saw, who
"ever it was, stopt to listen to our enchanting
"Notes—each Warbler was immediately silenced;
"whereupon, the Invader to our Melody, call'd
"out in a most rapturous Voice, 'Charming!
"Charming! proceed for *God* Sake, or I go Home
"directly'—no sooner were those Words uttered,
"than all as with one Consent sprung from their
"Seats, and ye Air eccho'd with 'pray, walk in my
"Lord;' No—indeed he would not, he would set
"on the Step's too; so after a few Ha, Ha's, and
"being told what all knew—that it was a delight-
"full Evening, at his desire we strew'd the Way
"over with Flowers &c &c till a full half Hour was
"elaps'd when all retir'd to their respective
"Homes..."

YET, despite such Displays of social Serenity, the political Rancour beneath them seemed to be bringing forth the Fruits of Redress. For, soon after his Dissolution of the Assembly, Lord *Botetourt* was assured by the *British* Secretary of State that further Duties would not be levied upon the Colonists, and, further, that those which had been imposed would be repealed. Thus, his Excellency summoned a new Assembly to announce this happy News; but, when it convened in *November* of the Year 1769, *Botetourt* found that the Assurances which had been given him were not yet fulfilled. Whereupon, his Lordship informed the Assembly of the Promise which was made to him and concluded in this Wise:

" . . . It may possibly be objected that, as his
" Majesty's present Administration are not im-
" mortal, their Successors may be inclined to at-
" tempt to undo what the present Ministers shall
" have attempted to perform; and to that Objec-
" tion I can give but this Answer, that it is my
" firm Opinion that the Plan I have stated to you
" will certainly take Place, and that it will never
" be departed from, and so determined am I for-
" ever to abide by it, that I will be content to be
" declared infamous, if I do not to the last Hour of
" my Life, at all Times, in all Places, and upon all
" Occasions, exert every Power with which I either
" am or ever shall be legally invested, in order to
" obtain and maintain for the Continent of *America*
" that Satisfaction which I have been authorized
" to promise this Day, by the confidential Ser-
" vants of our gracious Sovereign, who, to my cer-
" tain Knowledge, rates his Honour so high, that
" he would rather part with his Crown than pre-
" serve it by Deceit."

AND it is said that, the Tax upon Tea being continued, his Lordship proposed to resign his Commission; but was prevented by a great Illness

which came upon him. And as to this last, it has
been told that prior to his fatal Sickness, he was
visited at the Palace by *Robert Carter Nicholas*,
Esq., the Treasurer of the Colony; who remarked
to him that he, of all Men, should be most unwilling to die—he being so social in his Nature, so
greatly beloved, and surrounded by so many good
Things ministering to his every Whim and Com-
fort. Remembering these Words when he lay
upon his Death-bed, Lord *Botetourt* summoned
Nicholas to him, and, when that Gentleman en-
quired what he desired, his Lordship in a calm
Voice answered, "Nothing, but to let you see that
"I resign those good Things which you formerly
"spoke of with as much Composure as I enjoyed
"them."

Botetourt died on *October* 15, 1770, and with
general Mourning and the greatest Solemnity his
Remains were laid at rest in a Vault beneath the
Chancel of the Chapel of the College, which Institution he had ever favoured in Word and Deed.
And it is small Wonder that to the Honour of such
a Man the General Assembly of *Virginia* reared a
splendid Statue upon the Piazza of the Capitol,
which Statue, in this present Day, stands before
the great Building of the College. Upon opposite
Sides of its Pedestal appear the following Inscriptions; and these Inscriptions, in themselves, will
explain to Readers the otherwise strange Fact that
the *Virginia* Assembly appropriated Funds for the

Care and Cleaning of this Statue of his Excellency, even in the Midst of those fevered Years of the War of Revolution which were to come:

DEEPLY IMPRESS'D WITH THE WARMEST SENSE OF GRATITUDE FOR HIS EXCELLENCY THE RIGHT HONB^LE LORD BOTETOURT'S PRUDENT AND WISE, ADMINISTRATION, AND THAT THE REMEMBRANCE OF THOSE MANY PUBLIC AND SOCIAL VIRTUES, WHICH SO EMINENTLY ADORN'D HIS ILLUSTRIOUS CHARACTER, MIGHT BE TRANSMITTED TO LATEST POSTERITY, THE GENERAL ASSEMBLY OF VIRGINIA ON THE XX DAY OF JULY ANN: DOM: M, DCC, LXXI RESOLVED WITH ONE UNITED VOICE, TO ERECT THIS STATUE TO HIS LORDSHIP'S MEMORY.

———

LET WISDOM AND JUSTICE PRESIDE IN ANY COUNTRY; THE PEOPLE WILL REJOICE AND MUST BE HAPPY.

AMERICA, BEHOLD YOUR FRIEND: WHO, LEAVING HIS NATIVE COUNTRY, DECLIN'D THOSE ADDITIONAL HONOURS WHICH WERE THERE IN STORE FOR HIM, THAT HE MIGHT HEAL YOUR WOUNDS, AND RESTORE TRANQUILITY AND HAPPINESS TO THIS EXTENSIVE CONTINENT: WITH WHAT ZEAL AND ANXIETY HE PURSUED THESE GLORIOUS OBJECTS, VIRGINIA, THUS BEARS HER GRATEFULL TESTIMONY.

T H E Honourable *William Nelson*, Esq., (as it has already been intimated) became the Acting Governor upon the Death of Lord *Botetourt*; he being the President of the Council. And he continued in this Capacity for near a Year's Time; during which Term there was Peace and Quietude in the Colony. The despised Revenues were now reduced to a Minimum and, it has been said, the whole Disturbance might have passed far into the Future, had these Affairs continued with the Mildness that they now for a brief Time enjoyed. But this was not to be.

❀ ❀ ❀

IN the Fall of the Year 1771, *John Murray*, Earl of *Dunmore*, arrived in *Virginia* to be the full and resident Governor. And of this Executive it were next to an impossible Thing to give a fair and true Appraisal; for any Man who followed after *Dunmore's* deceased Predecessor could expect only to lose much or little by Comparison. Moreover, at the Palace in *Williamsburg*, *Dunmore* succeeded a Line of Governors who, in more favourable Times, had shown themselves to be Men as able, liberal, and assiduous as ever ruled a *British* Colony. Nor can it be denied that this new Governor faced Conditions and Events more violent and more hopeless than had any of his Predecessors. So that, if the *Virginia* Colonists looked upon *Dunmore* as a Man imperious and vindictive, their Judgement should now be tempered with Insight.

AT *Dunmore's* first Coming and for some Time thereafter, Things continued quietly in *Virginia*. If there was a Spirit of Refractoriness and a Yearning for Independence, it appeared not upon

THE ALTERNATIVE OF WILLIAMSBURG

Shewing either the Burgesses forced by their Constituents
to the signing of an Agreement of Non-Importation;
or else the Loyalists forced to such an Association
by the Sentiment of the aroused and angry Publick

From an Engraving done at London, 1775.

the Surface, but in Signs such as that discussed by the Honourable *William Nelson* in a Letter to a Correspondent in *London*, which went as follows:

" I now wear a good Suit of Cloth of my Son's
" Wool, manufactured, as well as my Shirts in
" *Albemarle & Augusta* Counties; my Shoes, Hose,
" Buckles, Wigg & Hat &c., of our own Country:
" and in these we improve every Year in Quantity
" as well as Quality."

YET, if the Colonists were now determined to pursue a Course of " Decency, Duty, and Re-" spect " in seeking their Objectives, it would seem that his Excellency was not able thus to disguise his Humour, for in *September*, 1772, the following appeared in the *South Carolina Gazette:*

" In *Virginia* their new *Scotch* Governor began
" his Government with Negligence and Disregard
" to the Duties of his Office. His Lordship was
" hardly ever visited, very difficult of Access and
" frequently could not be spoken with, when the
" most urgent Business of the Public called for his
" Attendance. These spirited Colonists could not
" bear these haughty Airs, but deputed one of their
" Lawyers to remonstrate against this supercilious
" Behavior, so inconsistent with the Service of the
" great Prince whom he represented. At first he
" stormed, but at last he agreed to name Office-
" Hours, when every Person concerned might at-
" tend on Business. Since which Time all Things
" have gone on very peaceably, and his Lordship
" has become much more tractable, to the Honour
" of his Master, and the great Advantage of the
" important Colony he presides over. Thanks to
" the true *American* Spirit of Liberty."

[65]

AND peaceably Things continued until the Assembly, which had been held prorogued for some Time, convened in *March* of the Year 1773. Then, a *British* Revenue Ship having been burned by Colonists in *Rhode Island* and it being noised about that the Perpetrators of this Deed would be sent to *England* for Trial, the Spirit of Revolt rose again in the House of Burgesses at *Williamsburg*. Upon the Gathering of the Assembly, *Thomas Jefferson*, *Patrick Henry*, *Richard Henry Lee*, *Francis Lightfoot Lee*, and *Dabney Carr* met together in a private Room of the *Raleigh* Tavern, and there they draughted Resolutions calling for the Appointment of a *Committee of Correspondence* to secure authentic Intelligences concerning the Actions of *Great Britain* and to communicate with the sister Colonies concerning such Things. And these Resolutions were offered in the House of Burgesses by *Dabney Carr* on *March* 12th, and, they being passed, brought about the Formation of similar Committees in the other Colonies. This Action, being looked upon by some Historians as the first successful Step toward a Uniting of the Colonies, has been considered the most significant Advance of the revolutionary Movement since the Resolutions against the *Stamp Act*.

LORD *Dunmore* now held the Assembly prorogued for more than a Year's Time, during which the *Committees of Correspondence* carried on a lively Exchange of Communications. Also during this Time occurred in *Massachusetts* that bold

Rebuke to *British* Taxation which has come to be known as the "*Boston Tea Party.*" And *Dunmore* had the Misfortune to have the *Virginia* Assembly in Session in *May*, 1774, when News was received at *Williamsburg* concerning the Act of Parliament which ordered the Sealing of the Port of *Boston* with an armed Force, the Embargo to become effective on *June* 1st of that Year. At once the Burgesses passed Resolutions protesting this Act and setting *June* 1st aside to be a Day of Fasting, Humiliation, and Prayer. (That this Resolve was adhered to is shown by the Diary of *George Washington*, who, for that Day, wrote: "Went to Church [*Bruton*] and fasted all Day").

AT this his Excellency dissolved the Assembly —but only to see them reassemble the following Day (*May* 27th) at the *Raleigh* Tavern, where some eighty-nine Burgesses entered into a general Association against the *East India* Company, and proceeded to the following important Recommendation:

"... We are further clearly of Opinion, that an "Attack, made on one of our sister Colonies, to "compel Submission to arbitrary Taxes, is an At- "tack made on all *British America,* and threatens "Ruin to the Rights of all, unless the united Wis- "dom of the Whole be applied. And for this Pur- "pose it is recommended to the *Committee of* "*Correspondence,* that they communicate, with "their several corresponding Committees, on the "Expediency of appointing Deputies from the "several Colonies of *British America,* to meet in

[67]

" general Congress, at such Place annually as shall
" be thought most convenient; there to deliberate
" on those general Measures which the united
" Interests of *America* may from Time to Time
" require."

AND, it being learned that the Sentiment in
favour of a general Congress was shared by several
other Colonies, *Virginia* took the Lead and the
Representatives of the People summoned the *First
Virginia Convention* to meet at *Williamsburg* for
the Purpose of electing Delegates to gather with
those of the other Colonies in such a general Congress. This Convention appointed *Peyton Randolph*, *Richard Henry Lee*, *George Washington*,
Patrick Henry, *Richard Bland*, *Benjamin Harrison*, and *Edmund Pendleton* to represent *Virginia*.
Of these *Peyton Randolph*, of *Williamsburg*, was
elected the President of the first Congress (which
convened at *Philadelphia* in *September*, 1774),
and *Patrick Henry* made his great Speech, in
which he declared that *British* Oppression had
effaced the Boundaries of the several Colonies.

YET, in the Course of these Things, Life proceeded at *Williamsburg* with the greatest Decorum
and Restraint. If the Citizens sent Cash and Provisions to the beleagured City of *Boston* in *Massachusetts*, they, on the other Hand, greeted the
Arrival of Lady *Dunmore* in their Midst (she and
her Children coming to join his Lordship) with
Bon-Fires, Illuminations and Rejoicing. And,
when her Ladyship, who was much respected, pre-

[68]

sented the Governor with a new Daughter at the Palace, the Rejoicing was such that the Infant, in return, was named *Virginia*.

❀ ❀ ❀

BY the Year 1775 the Dispute between *Great Britain* and the Colonies had come to such a Pass that an open War appeared to be inevitable. In *March* of that Year a second *Virginia* Convention was summoned, and, a *British* Man-of-War lying too close to *Williamsburg* for Conveniency, the Meetings were held in *St. John's* Church at *Richmond*. It was there (and not in *Williamsburg* as many have supposed) that *Patrick Henry*, on *March* 23rd, 1775, introduced his Bill for assembling and training the Militia. And, some Opposition arising from conservative Members, *Henry* carried his Motion with a great Oration, in the Course of which he said:

> " Is Life so dear, or Peace so sweet, as to be pur-
> " chased at the Price of Chains and Slavery? For-
> " bid it, Almighty *God!* I know not what Course
> " others may take, but as for me, give me Liberty
> " or give me Death!"

THE Action of the Convention brought about a decisive Act on the Part of the Governor, which precipitated the Outburst of Hostilities in *Virginia*. In a Letter to the *British* Secretary of State, written from *Williamsburg*, Lord *Dunmore* described this Event:

[69]

" The Series of dangerous Measures pursued by
" the People of this Colony against Government,
" which they have now entirely overturned, & par-
" ticularly their having come to a Resolution of
" raising a Body of armed Men in all the Counties,
" made me think it prudent to remove some Gun-
" powder which was in a Magazine in this Place,
" where it lay exposed to any Attempt that might
" be made to sieze it, & I had Reason to believe the
" People intended to take that Step. I accord-
" ingly requested of Lieut Collins, commanding his
" Majesty's armed Schooner the Magdalen, to con-
" vey the Powder on Board the Fowey, Man-of-
" War now on this Station, which that Officer,
" with a Party of his Seamen diligently executed;
" but tho' it was intended to have been done pri-
" vately, Mr Collins & his Party were observed, &
" Notice was given immediately to the Inhabitants
" of this Place; Drums were then sent thro' the
" City.—The independent Company got under
" Arms. All the People assembled, & during their
" Consultation, continual Threats were brought to
" my House, that it was their Resolution to sieze
" upon, or massacre me, & every Person found giv-
" ing me Assistance if I refused to deliver the Pow-
" der immediately into their Custody."

I T is both interesting and a significant Thing
that the Confiscating of the Powder at *Williamsburg,* thus described by Lord *Dunmore,* occurred
on the 20th Day of *April,* 1775; which was the
Day after the Battle at *Lexington* in *Massachusetts.* Concerning this, many have held it to be
but a strange Coincidence, while others have seen

in it a concerted Plan by which *Great Britain* had hoped to forestall an Outbreak of Rebellion in both Colonies. And, if this last were indeed the Case, the Failure of the Plan was tremendous; for when (in the short Space of nine Days) Word of the Affair at *Lexington* and *Concord* was received at *Williamsburg* (which was already virtually in Arms), a Broadside was issued by the *Virginia Gazette* closing with the Words, "The Sword is "now drawn, and *God* knows when it will be "sheathed."

N O R were the Disturbances which followed the Seizure of the Powder in *Virginia* confined to *Williamsburg* alone. For Troops were raised in various Places; and on *May* 3rd *Patrick Henry* appeared near the City with about one Hundred and fifty armed Men, gathered in a March from *Hanover*. These demanded the Return of the Powder or a Settlement for it; and the Governor found it necessary to comply with a Bill of Exchange for £330 before the Men would disperse.

T H E R E now followed at *Williamsburg* an eventful Period which is impossible of brief Description: The publick Treasury was held under the Guard of the angered Citizens. The Governor and the Assembly exchanged Communications in which the Sentiments of the Times were but poorly concealed. Dispatches from the Governor to the *British* Secretary of State (which were evidently seized or intercepted) appeared in the *Vir-*

ginia Gazette, as did such Items as the following, which furthered the unfriendly Spirit of the Times:

> "A Correspondent thinks it an odd Circum-
> "stance, that the *Cerberus* (whom the Poets feign
> "to be the three-headed Dog that guards the
> "Mouth of *Hell*) should be the Ship appointed to
> "carry over to *America* the three Generals ap-
> "pointed to tame the *Americans*."

LOYALISTS began to settle their Affairs and to leave the Colony. The Palace for some Time had been virtually an armed Fortress; and now, in the dark Hours of the Morning of *June* 8th, his Lordship and his Family fled from it to the Protection of the *Fowey* Man-of-War lying in the *York* River, the Governor fearing longer to try the Temper of the People. For a Time he sought to control the Government from the Safety of the Warship. But, failing this, and finding the Colonies to be in a State of open Rebellion (*George Washington* having taken Command of the Forces of the united Colonies on *July* 2nd) he set himself to making War upon the Colony he had lately governed. Then, suffering Reverses in this also, he sailed for *New York* and thence for *England*— and with him royal Authority departed forever from *Virginia*.

✿ ✿ ✿

IN the Time of the Interregnum the Government of *Virginia* devolved first upon the Assembly, and, when that Body adjourned its last active Session on *June* 24th, 1775, the Powers of

Government passed to the *Virginia Convention of Delegates* and to the *Committee of Safety* appointed by that Convention. The Convention also made *Patrick Henry* the Commander-in-Chief of all the *Virginia* Forces, and *Williamsburg* was appointed the Place for the Gathering of the Troops.

MEANWHILE, the House of Burgesses continued to convene in *Williamsburg* from Time to Time, but a sufficient Number of Members could never be gathered to enable the House to proceed to Business. And so it was that the Minutes of the Session called on *May* 6th, 1776, read:

" SEVERAL Members met, but did neither pro-
" ceed to Business, nor adjourn, as a House of
" Burgesses. FINIS."

THUS ended the *General Assembly* of *Virginia* that was composed of a *Council* and a *House of Burgesses*. It has since been advanced with Assurance to be the oldest representative legislative Institution in all *English America*; and by some (with devious Arguments) it has been shown to be the oldest in the World. For one Hundred and fifty-seven Years it had made the Laws for the *Virginia* Colony; and for at least one Hundred and fifty-three Years of this Time it had claimed and defended its sole Right to levy and approve Taxes upon *Virginians*. Now, in the Victory of this Principle, it passed away.

✿ ✿ ✿

[73]

ON *May* 6th, 1776, that same Day that the House of Burgesses ceased to exist, the fifth and, perhaps, the most memorable of the *Virginia* Conventions of Delegates met in the Capitol at *Williamsburg*.

I T so happened that a Number of Counties had now instructed their Delegates to declare for Independence (this Number including *Cumberland* County, which had directed its Delegates to " ab- " jure any Allegiance to his *Britannick* Majesty, " and bid him a good Night forever. ")   In Consequence of these Things, Resolutions were draughted, offered, and argued before a Committee of the whole House, directing the *Virginia* Delegates in the General Congress at *Philadelphia* to move that Body to declare the United Colonies to be free and independent States, and carrying the Assent of *Virginia* to such a Declaration. In these Proceedings, *Thomas Nelson*, Jr., *Patrick Henry*, *Meriweather Smith*, and *Edmund Pendleton* were conspicuous. The Resolutions, being presented to the Convention on *May* 15, 1776, by *Archibald Cary*, were unanimously passed. The Instructions of the Convention were fulfilled at *Philadelphia* by *Richard Henry Lee*, where they brought about the *Declaration of Independence*.

YET, *Virginia* did not wait upon the Results of her Motion in the General Congress to proceed in the Matter of Independence. For, on *June* 12th the Convention of Delegates approved a *Declaration of Rights*, which was for the most Part prepared by the Honourable *George Mason*, Esq., as a " Basis and Foundation of Government. " And, subsequently, on *June* 29th, the Convention unanimously adopted a *Plan of Government* (this also proceeding chiefly from the Pen of *George Mason*), which has been advanced as the first Constitution of a free and independent State. Thus, when the *Declaration of Independence* was signed at *Philadelphia*, *Virginia* already existed as an Independency. By its Constitution a new General Assembly had been formed, it consisting of a *House of Delegates* and a *Senate*, and this Assembly governs the *Commonwealth* of *Virginia* to this present Day.   ❀ ❀ ❀

U NDER the new Constitution *Patrick Henry* became the first Governor of the Commonwealth, he being chosen by the Convention upon its first Ballot. And soon he took up his Residence at the Governor's Palace, which, the Effects of Lord *Dunmore* having been disposed of at publick Auction, was now newly fitted out for his Use. And it has been told that some Men of Prominence and Fashion in that Time feared that *Henry's* Plainness of Appearance would not lend itself to the great Dignity of his new Office; but, it has further been told that he who in a former Day had ridden into *Williamsburg* upon a lean Horse and in poor Attire, now rose handsomely above all Expectations—he appearing at the Palace in a fine black Suit, a scarlet Cloak, and a Wig as great as any in the Country.

NOW, in *Henry's* Time as Governor, the War continued apace. With its Successes and Reverses the Tenour of Life in *Williamsburg* rose and fell; so that there were Times of Celebration and Times of Grief. The Hostilities, in which *Virginia* joined with all her Strength and Resources, raged to the North of her Boundaries and then to the South of them. News of the Surrender of *Burgoyne* in the North was received at *Williamsburg* with the greatest Rejoicing, as is indicated by the following Letter written by *John Page* of *Williamsburg* to General *Weedon:*

"... You relate the Battle with *Burgoyne*
"... We have had a *Feu de Joye* from our
"Troops, ringing of Bells and a grand Illumina-
"tion, and tho' it is now past 10 at Night the
"People are shouting and firing in Platoons about
"the Streets. ... I have been obliged to go down
"into the Streets and prevent a Riot and to pre-
"vail on my Neighbour *Lenox* to cease firing—
"who drunk as a Lord had been endeavoring to
"imitate a Cannon. ..."

IN the Year 1777 *Patrick Henry* and *George Rogers Clark* laid a Plan to carry a War of *Virginia's* own into her Northwest Territory, and there to put an End to the Incursions of the *British* under *Henry Hamilton*, the Governor of the Northwest (who, from his inciting the *Indians* against the *Americans*, was called "the Hair-Buyer.") Twice *Clark* proceeded against Fort *Vincennes*, and, on the second Occasion, in the Winter of 1779, he captured not only the Fort, but

Hamilton also, who, being brought back to *Will-iamsburg*, languished for some Time in the Prison near the Capitol. Of his Arrival at *Williamsburg*, this unhappy Prisoner wrote the Following in his Journal:

"About Sunset reached *Williamsburg*, wet, "jaded, dispirited, forming Ideas of what Sort of "judicial Examination I was to undergo. By the "Time we reached the Palace as it is called, the "Governor's Residence, our Escort of curious Per-"sons had become very numerous. The Officer "went in to give Account of his Mission, and we "remained on Horseback before the Door expect-"ing the Civilities naturally to be looked for from "a Man in first Place in the Province. In half an "Hour not finding our Expectations answered, I "flung myself from my Horse fatigued and morti-"fied to be left a Spectacle to a gazing Crowd. We "were however soon relieved from the painful "State of Uncertainty by the Appearance of the "Officer, who conducted us to the common Prison, "distant a small Mile, our Attendants increasing "every Step. At the Jail we were received by the "Jailer, a Character, however beneath other "People's Notice, which soon called our At-"tention. . ."

IN *June*, 1779, *Thomas Jefferson* succeeded *Patrick Henry* as the Governor of the *Virginia* Commonwealth. And now, in *Jefferson's* Time, the Proposal to move the Seat of *Virginia* Govern-ment to a more central Situation was again ad-vanced, as it had been some thirty Years before. The Measure found great Favour in the Eyes of the new Governor, who, being a Resident of

[77]

Albemarle, could well understand the Justice of the Notion. Moreover, *Williamsburg's* Accessibility to the Enemy in a Time of War entered into the Discussion; so that on *June* 12th, 1779, the Assembly was prevailed upon to pass an Act for removing the Seat of Government to *Richmond* (the Group of small Villages which composed that Place being looked upon as a Town "more safe " and central than any other Town situated on " navigable Water.") The Removal of the Offices of Government was effected in the opening Months of the Year 1780.

❀ ❀ ❀

THE Passing of the Seat of Government brought the Close of another Epoch in the History of *Williamsburg*. For near a Century and a Half it had now been looked upon as the " Heart and Centre " of *Virginia*—literally at the first and figuratively at the last. In this Time other Cities and Towns had grown up in *Virginia*, and some had surpassed *Williamsburg* in Growth and Size; but it is safe to say that, until the Removal of the Government, no City in all *America* had surpassed this Capital in its Influence and Accomplishment. For, as *Jamestown* had led *Virginia* through the Perils of Conquest and Settlement, so *Williamsburg* led that Colony through Times of Establishment and Expansion—and on to Liberty.

N o w it was to rest from these Labours.

A BRIEF & TRUE REPORT
CONCERNING
WILLIAMSBURG
in VIRGINIA

CHAPTER III.

WILLIAMSBURG was now to rest; yet, at the first, its Quiet was but short-lived. Gone from it were the Commotions of Publick Times, the Solemnities of the high Courts, the Fire and Fervour of political Debate, and all the Display and Ceremony of Government. But, in their Stead, the War moved into the Confines of the City; so that the Passing of the Seat of Government was near forgotten.

WITH the Beginning of the Year 1781, the *British* commenced a mass Invasion of *Virginia*, that Commonwealth being known to be but poorly equipped to resist such an Attack. *Virginia's* Resources were now near Exhaustion; and her Men and Guns were scattered in the Defense of her Sister States to the North and South. It has been said that the *British*, in Consequence of these Things, looked forward to an easy Campaign by which, through the Subjection of this central and important "Colony," they might break the Strength and Spirit of the Union arrayed against them.

Benedict Arnold now entered *Virginia* in Command of a *British* Force, and these Troops were later joined and augmented by a Force under General *Phillips*. Together these two ravaged the eastern Parts of *Virginia* at their Leisure; they being resisted at the first by small Bands of Militia, and later by an inferior Number of *American* Regulars sent by General *Washington* under the Command of the Marquis *de Lafayette*. After the Death of General *Phillips* at *Petersburg* (he dying of the Fever) the *British* Force was greatly increased by the Arrival of Troops from the South commanded by Lord *Cornwallis*, and that General then assumed Command of the united Forces, which numbered about seven Thousand.

THERE now followed a Series of Maneuvers and Stratagems in which *Cornwallis* sought to engage the vastly inferior Force under *Lafayette* in Battle. Failing in this, the *British* retired down the *Virginia* Peninsula, followed at some Distance by the *Americans*. On *June* 25th, 1781, *Cornwallis* entered into *Williamsburg* and encamped there for ten Days.

N o w there was Plundering and Famine in the City; Slaves were confiscated; the Small-pox was spread Abroad; and a Swarm of Flies (as dense as the Gloom that pervaded the Place) settled upon *Williamsburg*. *Cornwallis* established his own Headquarters in the House of the President of the College, leaving that Official to find Shelter elsewhere. The Price of Liberty now seemed dear indeed.

O n *July* 4th the *British* moved out of the City and, having administered a sharp Defeat to *Lafayette* near *Jamestown*, they crossed the River and proceeded to their Base at *Portsmouth*, from whence they later moved by Water to *Yorktown*.

I n *September* the Scene at *Williamsburg* was altered mightily; for then had begun that great Maneuver of the *American* and *French* Forces, together with the *French* Fleet, which brought about the Capture and Surrender of the *British* at *Yorktown*. And as this Affair drew on, *Williamsburg* became the Place for the Massing of the *French* and *American* Forces, while the *British* lay behind their Fortifications on the *York*. The Arrival of General *Washington* in *Williamsburg* was described by Colonel *St. George Tucker*, a Resident of the City and an Officer of the *Virginia* Militia, in this Fashion:

"I wrote you Yesterday that General *Washing-*
"*ton* had not yet arrived. About four o'Clock in
"the Afternoon his Approach was announced.
"He had passed our Camp, which is now in the
"Rear of the whole Army, before we had Time to

" parade the Militia. The *French* Line had just
" Time to form. The *Continentals* had more Lei-
" sure. He approached without any Pomp or
" Parade, attended only by a few Horsemen and
" his own Servants. The Count *de Rochambeau*
" and General *Hand,* with one or two more Officers
" were with him. I met him as I was endeavoring
" to get to Camp from Town, in order to parade
" the Brigade; but he had already passed it. To
" my great Surprise he recognized my Features and
" spoke to me immediately by Name. General
" *Nelson,* the Marquis, etc., rode up immediately
" after. Never was more Joy painted in any Coun-
" tenance than theirs. The Marquis rode up with
" Precipitation, clasped the General in his Arms,
" and embraced him with an Ardor not easily de-
" scribed. The whole Army and all the Town
" were presently in Motion. The General, at the
" Request of the Marquis *de St. Simon,* rode
" through the *French* Lines. The Troops were
" paraded for the Purpose, and cut a most splendid
" Figure. He then visited the *Continental* Line.
" As he entered the Camp the Cannon from the
" Park of Artillery and from every Brigade an-
" nounced the happy Event. His Train by this
" Time was much increased; and Men, Women
" and Children seemed to vie with each other in
" Demonstrations of Joy and Eagerness to see
" their beloved Countryman. His Quarters are at
" Mr. *Wythe's* [*George Wythe's*] House. Aunt
" *Betty* [Mrs. *Peyton Randolph*] has the Honor
" of the Count *de Rochambeau* to lodge at her
" House. We are all alive and so sanguine in our
" Hopes that Nothing can be conceived more
" different than the Countenances of the same Men
" at this Time and on the first of *June.* The Troops
" which were to attend the General are coming

[82]

"down the Bay—a Part, if not all, being already
"embarked at the *Head of Elk*. *Cornwallis* may
"now tremble for his Fate, for Nothing but some
"extraordinary Interposition of his Guardian
"Angels seems capable of saving him and the
"whole Army from Captivity."

❁ ❁ ❁

A DESCRIPTION of the Happenings at
Yorktown belongs to the History of that
Place, and not to a Report of this Nature. *Williamsburg* saw the Gathering of the Troops and the
Planning of the Siege. It saw the allied Forces
march out with their Flags waving; and it saw the
Wagons return bearing the *American* Wounded to
their Hospital at the Governor's Palace, and the
French Casualties to the Great Building of the
College. Following that memorable Day, *October* 19th, when the *British* laid down their Arms,
it saw the victorious Armies march back, and there
was Cheering and a Firing of Salutes. Indeed,
some of the *French* Troops were now quartered at
Williamsburg, and wintered there.

T H E Peace with *Great Britain*, the provisional
Articles of which were signed at *Paris* in *November*, 1782, was proclaimed at *Williamsburg* on
May 1st, 1783, with great Ceremony. The Order
of the Procession and Celebration for that Day
was announced as follows:

"1st Two Attendants in front, supporting two
"   Staffs, decorated with Ribbons, &c., &c.
"2d The Herald mounted on a Gelding neatly
"   caparisoned.

[83]

" 3d Two Attendants, as at first.
" 4th Sergeant bearing the Mace.
" 5th Mayor, Recorder, with Charter.
" 6th Clerk, behind carrying the Plan of the City.
" 7th Aldermen, two and two.
" 8th Common Council, in the same Order.
" 9th The Citizens in the same Order.

  " T H E Citizens to be convened on *Thursday* at
" 1 o'Clock at the Court House by a Bell Man.

  " A F T E R the Convention of the Citizens they
" are to make Proclamation at the C : House, after
" which the Bells at the Church, College & Capitol
" are to ring in Peal.

  " F R O M the C^t House the Citizens are to pro-
" ceed to the College, and make Proclamation at
" that Place, from whence they are to proceed to
" the Capitol and make Proclamation there; and
" from thence proceed to the *Raleigh* & pass the
" Rest of the Day."

A N D now the Quiet returned.

✿ ✿ ✿

SOME Observers have held that, with the Passing of the War, *Williamsburg* fell into a
Sleep; while Others have protested that it was not
a Sleep, but a Soliloquy (which is a Talking to
one's Self). The Population fell away; for many
of the Tradesmen now followed the Government
to *Richmond*. Yet, many of the established Families continued their Residence; so that for more
than a Century Travellers have been moved to
remark on the genteel Society and the Hospitality
of the Place.

[84]

THE College, with brief Interruptions, had continued in Operation through the Revolution (it had, in Fact, been made a University in the Year 1779). Now, with the Seat of Government removed, the Revenues from the Crown cut off, and the Support of the *English* Church lost to it, the College struggled on under the Guidance of its Presidents and Professors. The Lands granted by the Crown were yet held, and, indeed, the College Holdings were now increased by the Gift of the Palace Lands and other publick Lands, presented by the Assembly. Chiefly upon Proceeds from the Renting or Sale of these the College continued.

THE Palace no longer stood, it having been mysteriously burned while serving as an Hospital in 1781. Now the Capitol commenced to fall into Ruin, so that in 1794 the eastern Half was demolished and the Materials sold to defray the Expenses of maintaining the other Half (and that remaining Half was destroyed by a Fire in 1832).

FROM Time to Time *Williamsburg* rose again to Prominence upon brief Occasions; such, for Example, as that upon which *Lafayette* (who was in the Country as the Guest of the Congress) returned to the City in the Year 1824. The great *French* General was entertained at the Residence of Mrs. *Mary Monroe Peachy* upon the *Court House Green*, where he received an Ovation from the Citizens; following which, he was banqueted at the *Raleigh* Tavern. But such Events became increasing Rare, and the Interludes of Peacefulness the longer.

[85]

IN the Year 1827, a new Professor at the College described the Post Office at *Williamsburg* in a Letter to a Friend; and, the Post Office being a fair Indication of the Temper of any Town in that Time, the Letter is here set down:

" . . . I thought I was transported to *Noah's* "Ark, when I first came into this Town, so pro- "digious was the Quantity of Animals I met with, "without seeing a single Person till I reached the "Post Office which stands in the Center of Main "St. It is one of the Curiosities of this Place. I "wish I could describe it to you, but such Thing is "entirely out of my Power, and I defy *Walter* "*Scott* himself to do it, notwithstanding his aston- "ishing Imagination, but as to enable you to form "an incorrect Idea of this superb Establishment I "will tell you that there is not Article whatever in "the World which could not be found in it. It is a "Book Seller's Store in which you will find Hams "and *French* Brandy; it is an Apothecary's Shop "in which you can provide yourself with black silk "Stockings and shell Oysters; it is a Post Office in "which you may have Glisters, chewing Tobacco "*&* in a Word it is a Museum of natural History "in which we meet every Afternoon to dispute "about the Presidential Election, and about the "Quality of *Irish* Potatoes. . . . "

THE Houses and Buildings of the City continued to mellow with Years; and some of the older Structures (together with those that were unoccupied) commenced to fall into Ruin. From Time to Time a Building would fall a Prey to

Flames; and, more rarely, a new Building would rise, to shine forth in the Manner of a fresh Patch upon a well-worn Garment.

IN the Year 1838, *Bruton* Church became the Prey, not of Flames, but of a Church Fair, by which a considerable Sum was raised for the Repair and Modernizing of its Interior. In 1859 the Great Building of the College burned, and, though it was at once rebuilt, it lost the Handsomeness and Dignity with which Sir *Christopher Wren* and Colonel *Spotswood* had blessed it. In the same Year the *Raleigh* Tavern, which in Addition to its Guests, had for some Years housed Memories perhaps more momentous than those of any *American* Hostelry, fell also to Flames.

YET, *Williamsburg* continued in its philosophical Serenity—which some mistook for Slumber.

❀ ❀ ❀

THE Quiet and Serenity of *Williamsburg* were shattered in the Year 1861 by the Outbreaking of the *War Between the States*. And at once the Men and Boys of the City (including the Students, Professors, and the President of the College) distributed themselves to the Armies of the *Confederacy*.

IT would appear that it was almost an inevitable Thing that the War should come to *Williamsburg*; and, in the Year 1862, it came. From its first Foundation the City had been recognized and noted as a strategic and defensible Spot; and now it lay between a *Federal* Stronghold (*Fortress Monroe*) at the Foot of the Peninsula, and the *Confederate* Capital (*Richmond*) at the Head of it. And so it was that in *April*, 1862, General *George B. McClellan* advanced up the Peninsula with a *Union* Force numbering above a Hundred Thousand Men. He was met at *Yorktown* by a small *Confederate* Force, under Major General *J. Bankhead Magruder*. And while the *Federals* were held in check at *Yorktown*, *Magruder* threw a second Line of Redoubts, Rifle Pits, and a Barricade of Trees across the Peninsula on the eastern Outskirts of *Williamsburg*, with a Fort at the commanding Center of the Line. Then *Confederate* Reinforcements began to arrive; General *Joseph E. Johnston* appeared and took Command, and Generals *Early*, *Jones*, and *Hill* came up with reinforcing Divisions.

O N *May* 3rd *McClellan* was ready to fight at *Yorktown*, but the *Confederates* quietly fell back to the Fortifications at *Williamsburg*. *Johnston* now placed General *Longstreet* in Command of the Field for the *Confederates*. The Battle of *Williamsburg* was fought on *May* 5th, and the Homes, Churches, and publick Buildings of the City were filled with Wounded and Dying. Certain Citizens of *Williamsburg* ventured out beneath their Umbrellas (for it was raining) to watch the Battle at close Hand; but, becoming involved in the Retreat of a *Confederate* Company, they retreated also.

[88]

AT Nightfall (as previously planned) the Southern Forces fell back in good Order towards *Richmond*; and the *Federals* took Command of the City, resting at *Williamsburg* for several Days. Both Sides claimed the Victory and, the Question being a close one, most Historians of the War have been content to leave the Point undecided.

THE Campaign moved on to *Richmond*, where the Assault of the *Federals* was successfully resisted. Whereupon, many of *McClellan's* Troops marched back through *Williamsburg*; but the City continued in the Possession of the *Union*, and (with the Exception of one Day) served as an unwilling Outpost of the *Federal* Army throughout the remaining Years of the War.

IN *September*, 1862, a Band of *Confederate* Cavalry, under the Command of General *Wise*, recaptured *Williamsburg* and held it for one Day; they captured also the *Federal* Provost Marshall, who had made himself somewhat unpopular with the Citizens. Yet, in the Evening the City (but not the Provost Marshall) was retaken by the *Federals*; and, in Retaliation, certain Soldiers from the Rank and File of the 5th *Pennsylvania* Cavalry fired the Great Building of the College.

NOR was the College the only Building to suffer during this Period of Occupation. For many untenanted Dwellings were dismantled or torn down for Fire-wood; and the old Offices of the Palace (which had survived the Fire which destroyed that Building in 1781) were now taken down, that the Bricks might be used for the Chimneys of Officers' Huts. And through these Times the Citizens of *Williamsburg* continued so loyal to the Cause of the South that, in the Year 1863, it became necessary for the *Federal* Provost Marshall to threaten to place outside the Lines all those who would not take an Oath of Allegiance to the *Union*. Yet, this Threat was but partially fulfilled; for after a Number of Citizens were marched out of the City they were permitted to return, it becoming apparent that their Determination could not be changed by such Measures.

BUT these things passed with the Surrender at *Appomattox* on the 9th Day of *April*, 1865.

❀ ❀ ❀

WITH the Ending of the War the Quiet again resumed at *Williamsburg*; but it was a Quiet not of Peace alone, but also of Poverty. The Story of the Days of Reconstruction in the South is a familiar one. The Dwellings of the colonial Times and of the early Days of the *Republic* continued in Use now, not only because they were held in high Esteem, but also because the Funds necessary for their Replacement or even their Repair were rare indeed. The Slaves (happily) were gone; but the pleasant and symmetrical Gardens that they had tended now fell to Weeds and Ruin. Yet, Fish and Game might still be taken, and some Corn would spring from a Soil exhausted by the Culture of Tobacco; so that the same genteel Families lived on at *Williamsburg*.

THOUGH the Great Building of the College was lying in Ruins, the Institution resumed Exercises on a somewhat limited Scale in 1865; and in 1869 it was operating with a full Complement of Professors, and with its principal Building again in Use. Yet, in 1881 (on Account of a Lack of Funds) its Activities were again suspended, and they were not resumed until 1888, when Assistance was gained from the Commonwealth. In 1893, the College was indemnified in Part by the *Federal* Government for its Losses in the *War Between the States*. Ultimately (in 1906), the College passed into the Ownership of the Commonwealth.

THESE trying Times in *Williamsburg* were recently and ably described by the Honourable *George P. Coleman*, a Mayor of the City, in this Fashion:

" . . . *Williamsburg* on a Summer day! The
" straggling Street, Ankle deep in Dust, grateful
" only to the Chickens, ruffling their Feathers in
" perfect Safety from any Traffic Danger. The
" Cows taking Refuge from the Heat of the Sun,
" under the Elms along the Sidewalk. Our City
" Fathers, assembled in friendly Leisure, following
" the Shade of the old Court House around the
" Clock, sipping cool Drinks and discussing the
" Glories of our Past. Almost always our Past!
" There were Men and Women who strained every
" Nerve, every Means in their Power, to help the
" *Williamsburg* of the present Day, to supply the
" Necessities of Life to poorer Neighbors, to build

" up the College and procure Means of Education
" for their Children, but even they shrank from
" looking toward the Future. The Past alone held
" for them the Brightness which tempted their
" Thoughts to linger happily . . ."

A N D in this Fashion *Williamsburg* continued, a
quiet, thoughtful Center of Education and County
Government. Nor did it alter greatly until a Time
well into the twentieth Century.

✿ ✿ ✿

I N the Year 1903, a new Minister, the Reverend
William Archer Rutherfoord Goodwin, assumed the Rectorship of *Bruton Parish* Church.
And he (becoming interested in the fine History
of his ancient Charge) set about to raise a considerable Sum of Money for the Repair of that
Structure and for the Restoration of its interior
Appearance, which (as has been already stated)
was greatly altered in 1839. This Work was
brought to Completion in the Year 1907.

S O M E Years later, after a long Absence from
the City, this same Doctor *Goodwin* resumed his
Rectorship at *Bruton* Church; whereupon, in
1926, the ancient Residence of the Honourable
George Wythe, Esq. (the Teacher of *Jefferson*,
Marshall, *Monroe*, and many others) was purchased and restored, it becoming the Parish House
of *Bruton* Church.

B U T the Salvage and Restoration of a Church
and a single Dwelling could not stem the Tide

[92]

which had now set in, nor could the splendid Labours of the *Association for the Preservation of Virginia Antiquities* (which Association had now for some Time preserved the Powder Magazine and protected the Site of the ancient Capitol) stem this Tide. The World War with its fevered Activities and Results brought the twentieth Century to *Williamsburg* in great and generous Measure; for the City, because of its geographical Position, had ever stood in the Path of Wars. The Peninsula now became a Center for the Concentration of the Forces of the Army and the Navy, and for the Manufacture and Storage of Ammunition and Supplies. In Addition to this Activity, *Williamsburg* became the Base of Supplies for *Penniman*, a Town of some fifteen Thousand Inhabitants, which sprang up near by. This Town, which has since entirely disappeared, was especially created for the Making of War Munitions. Its sudden Growth brought about a Period of temporary Business Activity and Prosperity in *Williamsburg*. Properties changed Ownership rapidly. Enlargement of the City was contemplated and new Subdivisions were laid out.

As a Result of these Things the *Duke of Gloucester* Street became a teeming Highway of Concrete; great Posts to carry Wires and Cables were raised on every Hand; the empty Spaces in *Williamsburg*, which were the Sites of forgotten Buildings and Gardens, began slowly to be filled with Shops, and Stores, and with Stations for Gasoline. The old Houses and many of their Occupants resisted; but *Williamsburg*, with the Passing of the War, stood upon the Brink of a poor Success in a World of vast Accomplishment.

IN the Year 1924 Dr. *Goodwin* spoke before the *Phi Beta Kappa* Society in *New York* City concerning the College at *Williamsburg* and its historic Environment. Mr. *John D. Rockefeller*, Jr., was in Attendance at this Lecture, following which Dr. *Goodwin* invited him to visit *Williamsburg*. This Mr. *Rockefeller* did many Months later, in 1926, and in the Course of this Visit Dr. *Goodwin* presented and explained to him the Thought which had long been in his Mind of restoring the City to its colonial Appearance, and of preserving it both for the Future and from the Fate which then seemed imminent.

IN 1926 Mr. *Rockefeller* returned again to *Williamsburg* to attend the Dedication of a Hall memorial to the Founders of the *Phi Beta Kappa* Society at the College, and in the Course of this Visit the Preparation of preliminary Restoration Drawings was authorized. In the Year 1927 Mr. *Rockefeller* made the Decision to undertake the Fulfillment of Dr. *Goodwin's* Plan, which Plan was soon defined as " an Endeavor to restore ac- " curately and to preserve for all Time the most " significant Portions of an historic and important

"City of *America's* colonial Period." And this Plan and Endeavor are now fulfilled; so that the City which in the Year 1926 looked forward to a Future of little Promise has instead moved backward into the Protection of a Past which in the Annals of *American* History is unexcelled.

A BRIEF & TRUE REPORT
CONCERNING
WILLIAMSBURG
in VIRGINIA

CHAPTER IV.

T O the Minds of Many the *Williamsburg Restoration* will appeal principally as a Means to an End. To such Minds the Methods of the Work will be of small Concern, as compared with the Results and their Meaning. For these it will be sufficient that the Restoration is nearing material Accomplishment and that its inspiriting Processes have begun.

T o other Minds, more technical in their Interest, the Project will appeal not as a Means to an End alone, but also as an End in itself. And these will wish to know how the Work was done, as well as the Whys and the Wherefores of it.

THIS Chapter, then, can be directed to neither of these Types; for in one Case no Chapter is required, and in the other the Adherents will wish to await the detailed Reports and Publications which the Future, of Necessity, must bring as an Explanation and a Record. The Chapter is directed, rather, to those who lean neither to one Extreme nor the other; yet, in its Brevity, it is designed to give to those that do as little Displeasure as may be.

❀ ❀ ❀

THERE are those who hold, with little or greater Insight, that if History moves in Cycles, then Progress may be made along either of its Courses—and much Effort saved by those who but stand still.

WHEN its Restoration was undertaken, *Williamsburg* (as has been intimated) displayed abounding Evidence of the architectural Implications of this philosophical Confusion. In a few short Years it had ceased to be an isolated and pleasingly decayed colonial City. Outwardly it had become a Highway Town in which the Ancient and the Modern were mingled in an Effect of peculiar Aggravation.

THE early Plan of the City was unchanged, and, even in its makeshift Modernity, *Williamsburg* preserved a Proportion of its colonial Buildings which, in Relation to its eighteenth Century Size, was perhaps greater than that possessed by

[97]

any *English-American* colonial City. Yet, the intruding modern Buildings were substantial in Number, if, as in many Instances, they were unsubstantial in aesthetic Conception.

A THEATRE which now stood upon the Site of a colonial Dwelling evidenced its Safety from Flames, if not from the Advance of Time, in its Construction of unpainted galvanized Iron. A Garage, also of corrugated Iron, displayed on its rusted Doors a facetious Acknowledgment to Archaeology in the Form of a Sign reading "Toot- "an-kum-in"—in timely Recognition of the Opening of the Tomb of *Tutenkhamon*, a *Pharoah* of the fourteenth Century before *Christ*.

SOME thirty Structures of varying Purpose and Design, ranging from a National Bank to a Pig Sty, had crowded together upon the *Market Square*, obscuring the Powder Magazine and the Prison which had once commanded the southern Half of that ancient Common. At the Foot of the *Duke of Gloucester* Street the original Foundations of the Capitol were outlined by a Concrete Covering in a rolling Field of Weeds. Two School Houses, one a monstrous Structure, stood at the Head of the *Palace Green*, while a Dwelling of the *Victorian* Era closed what had been the Vista at its Foot. Two modern Brick Stores occupied the Site of the *Raleigh* Tavern. The Great Building of the College stood (after three Fires and as many Alterations) supported chiefly by Necessity and its own good Balance. On the new-columned Portico of the Court House of 1770 Orange-coloured Benches bore, in large black Letters, the hospitable Inscription " Rest here in a " *Garner* Suit. "

H E R E and there a leaning Dormer or a handsome Chimney Cap offered the only visible identifying Features which marked Instances in which colonial Buildings had been swallowed up in successive Renovations, Alterations, and Repairs. At Intervals appeared colonial Buildings which had been little changed or partially restored. Old Structures and new stood Side by Side in a Confusion in which each detracted from the other. The Concrete Sidewalks of the *Duke of Gloucester* Street were shaded by Trees, but its Center was lined with heavy Poles from which Wires and Cables radiated. There was a Beauty, too, of a Kind which cannot be gained by conscious Effort; but this was available only to those who, looking out of half-closed Eyes, were able to see those Things which they valued, to the Exclusion of all else.

S U C H , then, was the Dilemma which the City of *Williamsburg* presented in 1926. There was much of the Worst that was new; there was much of the Best that was old—very old.

❋ ❋ ❋

I N 1927 Mr. *Rockefeller* commissioned Dr. *Goodwin* to purchase the Property necessary to the Accomplishment of the Restoration. In the

Course of this buying Program, most of the Properties which had composed the more important colonial Areas of the City proper were acquired. Much of this Property was purchased outright, though in certain Instances Properties were purchased subject to the Life Right or Tenure of Individuals whose Age or whose Associations with the Properties made such Procedure desirable.

THE Areas thus secured were turned over to two Corporations which were now formed to carry the Undertaking forward. The *Williamsburg Holding Corporation* (now *Williamsburg Restoration*, Incorporated) became the administrative Organization in Charge of the Project and acquired Title to much of the Property which had been purchased. *Colonial Williamsburg*, Incorporated, was formed to hold Title to Properties traded or presented to the *Restoration* by the City of *Williamsburg*, the *Association for the Preservation of Virginia Antiquities*, and by individual Donors. This Corporation has since held Title to and managed Properties, Buildings, and Activities devoted and restricted to historical and educational Purposes. Colonel *Arthur Woods* was the first President of both Corporations.

MEANWHILE, the Firm of *Perry, Shaw & Hepburn*, Architects, was retained to have Charge of the architectural Development of the Plan; *Arthur A. Shurcliff* to have Charge of Landscape Restoration and the Work of City Planning; and the Firm of *Todd & Brown*, Incorporated,

Engineer-Contractors, to develop and control the Organization which executed the Plans developed by the Architects and Landscape Architects, when approved by the executive Corporations.

OPERATIONS were prefaced by exhaustive Studies of the City, in Order that those engaged in the Work might familiarize themselves with the practical Intricacies of the Problem before them. A complete Property, Utility, and Topographical Survey of the City was made, and a Map prepared which, so far as possible, recorded every Detail of Interest. Engineering Specialists were employed to study the Water System, sanitary System, and the Light and Telephone Facilities, in the Knowledge that these would have to be improved, extended, and obscured. A zoning Expert was retained to prepare Recommendations for Codes and Ordinances which would assure an ordered Development. Tree Surgeons were employed to protect and revive failing Vegetation. A Survey of Fire Prevention and Protection was made. Committees of Specialists and Authorities in many of the Fields involved were formed to aid in a critical and advisory Capacity. These included a Committee of Advisory Architects, a Committee of Landscape Architects, a Committee of Historians and Scholars, and several Committees on Decoration and Furnishings.

A T its Beginning, the *Restoration* was considered to be primarily an architectural Problem. In Consequence, a Division of Decoration was formed to serve under the Architects, as was a Department of Research and Record. Under the Department of Research and Record a Division of archaeological Investigation was established.

T H E Properties purchased within the colonial Area of the City were at first divided, roughly, into two Areas. One of these was designated for immediate Restoration, the other being looked upon at the Time as a protective Area, concerning the Restoration of which no Commitments were made. The first Endeavors were therefore confined to the more prominent colonial Sections of the City, including the original Yard and Buildings of the College, the full Length of the *Duke of Gloucester* Street, the *Capitol Square*, the *Market Square*, and the *Palace Green*.

W I T H I N the Area thus defined, the architectural Problems were classified under four general Types of Work:

I. The Removal of all modern Buildings.
II. The Restoration of existing and partially existing eighteenth Century Buildings and Outbuildings.
III. The Reconstruction of certain Buildings and Outbuildings which had disappeared.
IV. The Decoration of Buildings thus restored and reconstructed, and the Furnishing of those to be exhibited to the Publick.

THE first of these Divisions of the Work (the Demolishment of modern Buildings) has proved the simplest, though perhaps the most protracted and trying. At this present Writing, five Hundred and ninety-one modern Buildings have been torn down or moved from the Restoration Areas; and a few remain to be demolished or moved. Yet, throughout this Process the Ideal has been that in no Case should a Tenant be left without a Home, and that no Business should be asked to vacate its Quarters without the Offer of a new Location.

❀ ❀ ❀

THE Accomplishing of the second Division of the Work (the Repair and Restoration of existing colonial Buildings) was prefaced by a comprehensive and detailed Study of existing colonial Buildings throughout *Virginia*, especially in the *Tidewater* Section surrounding *Williamsburg*, and more especially within the City itself. This Study was made in Order that original structural Features and architectural Details which had been effaced by successive Repairs and Alterations might be replaced upon the Basis of definite contemporary sectional or local colonial Precedent.

AS to this, it should be pointed to that the eighteenth Century Buildings of *Williamsburg* and of its surrounding Countryside were built by a limited Number of Master Builders, Mechanics, Artisans, and their Apprentices, representing but a few Generations in Time and Tradition. Again, these Builders were to a considerable Degree limited by the Implements and Materials which were readily available. So that the judicious Use of contemporary Precedent was resorted to with more than reasonable Assurance of Authenticity.

MOREOVER, it should be noted that from its Findings the Research Department was frequently able to supply specific documentary and pictorial Evidences in Cases in which more tangible Indications were lacking.

BY such and similar Processes seventy-seven existing or partially existing early Buildings have been restored or extensively repaired up to the present Time.   ❀ ❀ ❀

WITH Regard to the third Division (the Reconstruction of colonial Buildings which had disappeared) the Solutions were attained through the foregoing Processes, as outlined, but with especial Emphasis laid upon the Evidences contributed by the Department of Research and Record and by its archaeological Division.

HERE it should be explained that the Department of Research and Record, throughout the first Years of its Activity, was concerned primarily and principally with the Collecting of Source Data relating to the architectural, landscape, and decorative Problems of the *Restoration*. In seeking this Type of Information, every conceivable Source of pertinent colonial *Virginiana* was untiringly investigated. Governmental Archives, military Records, and commercial Accounts were carefully studied. The Collections and Archives of Libraries, historical Societies, and Museums were searched. Family Records and personal and publick Papers in private Hands were sought out. Early Newspapers, old Insurance Policies, local Tax and Court Records were especially fruitful. Paintings, Prints, Sketches, Maps, and old Photographs were minutely studied. Such Investigations were conducted in every Section of this Country, and were pursued as assiduously in *England* and in *France*.

THUS, by Way of Example, in the Case of the Governor's Palace, the Department of Research and Record was able to provide a Report composed of more than three Hundred Pages of Source Material relating specifically to the Palace, its Grounds, Buildings, and outlying Lands. It was also able to provide Prints from a provably accurate Engraving in Copperplate (located in the *Bodleian* Library, *Oxford*, *England*, and afterwards presented by that Institution to Mr. *John D. Rockefeller*, Jr.) which depicted the principal Facade of the Palace, together with its flanking Offices and a Portion of its Gardens. This Information was further supplemented by a detailed Floor-plan of the Palace proper (located in the Collections of the *Massachusetts Historical Society*) drawn by *Thomas Jefferson*, who once lived in the Palace as the Governor of the *Virginia* Commonwealth.

I T should also be explained, in Connection with the Reconstruction of Buildings, that the archaeological Division of the Research Department located, excavated, and recorded Score upon Score of colonial Foundations, not only establishing the Location of early Buildings and Outbuildings, but also discovering from Evidences and Indications, and to varying Degrees, their Size, Plan, Purpose, and general structural Character. In this Work the so-called "*Frenchman's Map*," believed to have been drawn by a *French* Army Cartographer in 1782, was of inestimable Assistance. This Map, the original Draught of which is preserved in the Library of the *College of William and Mary*, presents the Plan of the City proper and outlines, roughly, the Shapes, relative Sizes, and Positions of its Buildings and many of their Outbuildings as they appeared at the Close of the *American* Revolution.

T H E Foundations thus located and excavated were, naturally, of primary and fundamental Importance to the Reconstruction of Buildings which had disappeared. Yet, it should be mentioned that, as successive Foundations were excavated, Ton after Ton of Objects and Fragments of Objects were recovered from the Earth removed from within and around them. Such excavated Relics provided not only contributory structural and architectural Evidences, but provided also, within obvious Limitations, a remarkable Record of the Life and Activities which the original

Buildings had sheltered. Viewed as a whole, the Collection, accumulated from so large a Number of Excavations of widely varying Types within a single Community, indicates Modes, Fashions, and general Trends, thus affording an interesting Insight into the social, domestic, and economic Life of the entire City and, to a Degree, of the Times.

To use the Palace again as an Example, archaeological Investigation revealed the entire original Foundation and Basement of the Palace proper, with its Stone Floor intact, and with its Partition Walls, Chimney Bases, Wine Bins, and vaulted Cellars existent or clearly indicated. Investigation also revealed the Foundations of its flanking Offices, its Outbuildings, Walls, Wall Piers, Gates, Garden Steps, Walks, Wells, arched Drains, and many other interesting and significant Indications of the early Plan of the Place.

In the Seeking out of such fundamental Information, loose Objects and Fragments encountered in digging, or screened from the Earth removed, provided a Variety of useful Knowledge, including: Indications of the general Calibre and Character of interior and exterior Hardware and of decorative wrought Iron; invaluable Evidences pertaining to the Design and Material of many Mantel-pieces, sculptured Mantel Panels, Fireplace Facings, Under-fires, Firebacks, and Hearth Stones; Evidences establishing certain Types of Stone Embellishment, such as Caps for Wall Piers and the Design and Detail of Entrance Steps;

[107]

Examples of Wall Copings, Paving Tiles, Water-table Bricks, ground or rubbed Bricks for Orna-mentation, Gutter Bricks, Well Bricks. Even a large Section of the original exterior Wall of the Palace was recovered, which Section had fallen intact and which established the Size of the Face Brick employed, the decorative Use of glazed-head Brick as the header Bricks laid in *Flemish* Bond, and established also the Texture of the Mortar and the Tooling of the Mortar Joints.

T H U S, with such extensive Information avail-able and with, in this Case, the Assistance of both *Virginia* and *English* Precedent (for the Building was unusually pretentious for the Colonies), it was possible for the Architects to evolve a Conception of the Palace which, it is believed, would be convincing to the colonial Governors themselves, could they return to look upon it.

A N D the Palace, while it is one of the major Accomplishments of the *Restoration*, is but one of one Hundred and eighty-eight Buildings which have been reconstructed on ancient Foundations in Reproduction of Buildings long or late destroyed.

✿ ✿ ✿

I N the Accomplishment of the fourth Division of the Work (the Decoration of restored and reconstructed Buildings, and the Furnishing of those to be exhibited to the Publick), the Archi-tects' Division of Decoration also had Recourse to the voluminous documentary Records assembled, to the specific and generalized Findings resulting from archaeological Investigation, and to the Use of *Virginia* and *English* Precedent.

T H E Question of Paint Colours for decorating Exteriors and Interiors presented a Problem of particular Subtilty. In the Case of existing Buildings, Information could often be had by scraping through successive Paint Coats, with a View to discovering the early Colours employed. A Wealth of similar Precedent was provided by the Investigation of Paint Coats on Buildings throughout the Section. Yet, if a true Appreciation was to be attained, it was necessary that these Colours be envisaged in their original Condition and Appearance, with the Effects of Age, Decay, Soilure, and of contiguous Coats discounted. Again, though explicit Records existed concerning particular Colours employed in certain of the restored and reconstructed Buildings, the Shades and Tones of these Colours had to be arrived at through studied Conjecture. When, as in the Majority of Instances, specific Records of Colour were lacking, the prevailing Practices of the Section and of the Period were pursued, these being established not only by the Examination of more or less defaced Examples of actual Paint, but also through the careful Study of import Manifests, Merchants' Advertisements, and the Orders for Paints, Pigments, and kindred Supplies placed by the Colonists with their *London* Agents. Thus, in the Solution of the Problem, it was necessary to bring to bear a Combination of Knowledge, Reason, and advised good Taste; for Partialities in Colour and Shade vary with Times, as they do with Peoples— and Colour, in itself, has been a Phenomenon which has sorely perplexed Artisans, Artists, and Philosophers in many Ages.

I T was, perhaps, in their Bearing upon Furniture, Furnishings, and Accessories that the documentary Records, as first assembled, made their most generous Contribution to the physical Restoration of *Williamsburg*. For these Records contained the Enumerations of a Time when a Man's cracked Punch-bowl, his Bolster, Bed-feathers, and Parcels of damaged Pewter were carefully itemized in the Inventory of his Estate—a Time when a Merchant would not spare the Mention of a Hat-pin or a Pound of Thread in advertising his latest Shipment just imported from *London*.

T H U S, when the Furnishing of the Palace was undertaken, two extensive Inventories were available, outlining not only the Belongings of two colonial Governors (*Fauquier* and *Botetourt*), who died while residing in the Palace, but also indicating the Distribution of these Belongings within the Building and its Offices. Moreover, one of the Inventories listed also the " Standing Furni- " ture " in the Palace, which was owned by the Colony and remained in the Building from one Administration to another.

F O R the Furnishing of the reconstructed Capitol, the precise Records of the Assembly were to be had from the Journals and Statutes of Government, these specifying the Furniture and Accessories required for the various Rooms, and ranging in their Detail to the Measurements of Tables, the Colour and Material of Table Carpets, and the Colour of the Tape and the Type of Nails to be used in upholstering the Benches in the Hall of the *House of Burgesses.*

I N the Case of the *Raleigh* Tavern, the detailed Inventories of two of its colonial Keepers existed, these indicating an Elegance which its unique Function and persistent Tradition demanded, and which its exacting Patronage required.

O N the Basis of such Records, contemporary Furniture and Furnishings were purchased in *Virginia*, in various other Sections of the *Atlantic* Seaboard, and in *England*, in Keeping with the Practice of the *Virginia* Colonists. Also many valued Gifts were received. In some Instances, original *Williamsburg* Pieces were traced and purchased; and yet others have been lent by the General Assembly of *Virginia.* In Cases in which old Pieces could not be had, careful Reproductions of contemporary Originals were made. This last Procedure was especially indicated in the Case of the Capitol, the original Furniture of which was doubtless for the most Part destroyed in the Fire of 1747, and was of a cumbersome, institutional Type not readily come by.

A G A I N , the detailed Findings and general Conclusions resulting from archaeological Investigation were of great Assistance. It is (or should be) common Knowledge among Antiquarians that the ordinary Possessions of the People of a given Age, while generally existing in great Quantity, are often accorded little Thought and less Care—and so survive in ever diminishing Numbers among the Possessions of their Posterity. Thus, in Time, these once-common Things may even come to be looked upon as the extraordinary, if they survive at all. On the other Hand, the unusual, the fine, the unique Possessions of that same Day, accorded at first the Protection of locked Cupboards and higher Shelves and later entrusted to the Keeping of Museums of Art and History, come in Time to be (and therefore seem) the more usual and representative Articles of the Time. Against such Distortions the Tons of stained and corroded Fragments recovered from the local Soil provide, for *Williamsburg*, an admirable Assurance. Here, within the Limitations of the Collection, are the Possessions of the Period, in Fact and in Proportion. Moreover, in the many Instances in which such tangible Evidences can be applied in Conjunction with documentary Records, a high Degree of Authenticity is attained; for then the " 2 Doz. large Plates " listed in an Inventory associated with a given Site become Plates of a specific Ware, Colour, and Design, and so it is with various other Types of household and general Paraphernalia.

BY such Methods, and by countless others too intricate and varied for Inclusion in Generalizations such as these, have the restored and reconstructed Buildings of *Williamsburg* been decorated, and its Exhibition Buildings refurnished. Many Buildings are privately tenanted, and others adapted to the Reception of the considerable Concourse of People who again resort thither; yet these, more often than not, are furnished by their Occupants after a Manner which their Decoration and Design all but demand. And other Buildings of every Type continue to materialize, as will be told.

❁ ❁ ❁

THE Problem of the Landscape Architect, while in many Ways less confined and technical than that of the structural Architects, was more obscure.

AS has been said, many of the Homes and Buildings of the colonial Period were preserved as a Matter of practical and physical Necessity throughout that increasing economic Depression which had pervaded *Williamsburg* since the Removal of the Seat of Government in 1780, and more especially since the *War Between the States*. On the other Hand, the Pleasure Gardens which had surrounded so many of these Buildings fell Victims not only to the Curtailment and Neglect commonly accorded Luxuries in such Times, but also to their own transitory Nature. Beyond this, and again by the very Nature of them, the physical

Evidences for Landscape Restoration were neither so numerous nor so clearly defined as those existing as a Basis for structural Restoration and Reconstruction.

IN some few Instances major Evidences and Indications of colonial Gardens had survived. More often, their Re-creation was of Necessity based upon documentary References or Descriptions, upon Precedents and Prints, and upon such Evidences as buried Brick Walks, long-used Paths, and the general Arrangement of the older Trees, surviving Shrubbery, and indicative Disturbances of the Terrain. And such Indications had, of course, to be inter-related with the Arrangement of surviving Buildings and ancient Foundations.

IN View of this Situation, and in Order that a Wealth of Precedent and a thorough Understanding of the Feeling of the Period might be developed, an extensive Survey was made of the distinguishing colonial Features surviving in the Design of the Gardens of the South and of Characteristics in the Design of *English* Gardens continuing from the eighteenth Century. A particularly intensive Study was made of contemporary Pictures, Plans, and Maps.

IN the Matter of Plantings, another careful Study was made of the History of native Trees, Shrubs, and Flowers, and of Records pertaining to the Importation of foreign Seeds, Plants, and Cuttings. Fortunately, the Writings and Records of both professional and occasional Botanists and

Horticulturists were voluminous, and the Exchange of Information between them habitual. So that it can be stated with Confidence that there are today no Plantings in the restored and re-created Gardens of *Williamsburg* which might not have existed in the colonial Gardens which they represent.

THE Question of City Planning confronted the Landscape Architect with the Problem of preserving the early Plan of the City (which had survived with but few Alterations), while meeting the Requirements of present-day Traffic. With the Cooperation of the Federal, State, and City Governments, new Routes, Roads, and Streets have been provided outside and underneath the restored Area in a Profusion which, though it may perplex the Uninitiated, will serve the increased Demands and Purposes of the Publick.

THE Landscape Architect and the structural Architects collaborated in the Removal of the outward or exterior Evidences of Modernity, and in the Replacing of them with the Appurtenances of colonial Times. Thus, again on the Basis of contemporary Records and Precedent, the Lampposts, Fences, Brick Walks, Street Surfaces, and other exterior Features of the colonial City have reappeared; though, in certain Instances, these have been adapted to the Demands of the present Age and to the Convenience and Conveyances of its People.

✿ ✿ ✿

AND of the foregoing major Types and Divisions of the Work of Restoration, planned and supervised by Architects, Engineers, Landscape Architects, Decorators, and Experts in many Fields, working under the Direction of the administrative Corporations, it should be noted that the physical Execution of it has been and is being accomplished, in generous Part, by an Organization of skilled Mechanics and Artisans, trained to the Methods of colonial Builders and versed in the peculiar and exacting Demands of Restoration Work. And though the Labourer, as the Scripture holds, is worthy of his Hire; yet, they that work in Advance of the normal Skills and Demands of their Crafts are worthy also of Admiration and Esteem.

❀ ❀ ❀

AT the Close of the Year 1934, after eight Years of intensive Work and the Expenditure of many Millions of Dollars, the *Williamsburg Restoration* was considered and announced to be formally complete. Over four Hundred modern Buildings had been demolished and one Hundred and fifty early Buildings had been restored or reconstructed. A new Business District, designed to be in Keeping with the restored Areas, had been provided. Wires had been placed Underground and Streets resurfaced. Four Exhibition Buildings, the Capitol, the Governor's Palace, the *Raleigh* Tavern, and the Court House of 1770

(containing the *Williamsburg Restoration Archaeological Exhibit*), had been opened to the Publick; and the Opening of the *Ludwell-Paradise*
House (containing Mrs. *John D. Rockefeller,
Junior's,* Collection of *American* Folk Art) was
pending. In *October* of that Year the President of
the *United States,* in Company with the Governor
of *Virginia,* officiated at the formal Opening of
the *Duke of Gloucester* Street and the Areas ad-
joining it.

Y E T, in the Passage of Time, it has turned out
that such Announcements and Ceremonies marked
not the Completion of the Restoration, but
marked, rather, the Beginning of a new Conception of it and of new Advances toward the Fulfillment of that broadened Conception.

A s first projected, the Intention of the *Restoration* had been to restore certain of the ancient and
historic Buildings surviving in *Williamsburg*
(thus saving them from impending Destruction or
Decay), to reconstruct certain other Buildings of
especial historical Interest, to landscape the
Grounds and Areas thus involved, and, with the
more modern and anachronistic Buildings removed, to preserve and present a Memorial indicative (or, at least, reminiscent) of the *English-
American* colonial Period. Thus, in the Minds of
Most, the ultimate Result was at first visualized as
an historical Center in which a generous Scatter-
ing of restored and reconstructed Buildings, interspersed with Gardens and landscaped Areas,

would exemplify the various architectural and structural Types which had existed in *Williamsburg*, and which would be generally remindful (though not fully representative) of the local colonial Scene.

As to this, and of these Years, the Following has been written of the Architects of the *Restoration:*

"Approaching the Work in a Belief that "perhaps it might require Buildings and Gardens "freely designed in the old Manner, the Archi-"tects, as the Soil and the old Records commenced "to give up their Secrets, became passionate his-"torical Students, happy to subordinate their "creative Abilities to a loyal Interpretation of the "ample Evidence discovered."

SIMILARLY, on the Part of Mr. *Rockefeller* and the administrative Corporations, it can be said that, as the Work advanced, countless new Actualities, Potentialities, and Possibilities for the Project as a whole became increasingly apparent; and that only out of the Experience and Knowledge gained from these opening Years could a broader Conception of the Restoration have developed.

IT is often difficult to date Processes of Thought and Decisions developing out of Experience. Let it suffice, then, to say that after a Period of Contemplation, in which the Revealments of its opening Years were weighed, the *Restoration* moved forward toward a Fulfillment more complete than could have been envisioned at the first.

❈ ❈ ❈

IN 1935, Mr. *Kenneth Chorley* became the President of *Williamsburg Restoration*, Incorporated, and *Colonial Williamsburg*, Incorporated. Long the Vice-President of both Corporations, and for some Time their acting President, he succeeded Colonel *Woods*, who became Chairman of the Boards and who subsequently retired because of ill Health. Colonel *Woods* was succeeded as Chairman of the Boards by Mr. *John D. Rockefeller*, III.

WITH an enlarged and extended Program decided upon, the various Divisions of the Work were at this Time integrated to center in a single Organization, operating under the immediate Direction of the administrative Corporations. The Architects and certain other Experts were retained in an advisory Capacity. But now the several Departments which had been continued, taken over, or formed for the Maintenance and Interpretation of the Project, became also the active Agencies for the Development and Supervision of its added Endeavors.

SUBSEQUENT to these Alterations of Plan and Organization, a Number of the wide Spaces which existed between the restored or reconstructed Buildings of the first Period of Restoration have gradually filled with yet other Buildings, thus offering a more complete Representation of a colonial Metropolis. Also new Areas have been added to those originally chosen for Restoration, and additional Properties have been purchased or

[119]

have become available within them all. Thus, during the past six Years one Hundred and thirty-one Buildings of modern or anachronistic Design have been added to those already demolished or removed from the Restoration Areas; one Hundred and four additional Buildings of the eighteenth Century have been reconstructed; and eleven colonial Buildings have been added to the List of those already restored.

MEANWHILE, two major Exhibition Buildings, the Publick Gaol and the *George Wythe* House (with its impressive though characteristic Complement of Outbuildings), have been added to those already open to the Publick. This Group has been further augmented by the Provision of a Cabinet-maker's Shop, a Smithy, a Pewterer's Shop, a Barber and Perukemaker's Shop, and a Boot and Shoemaker's Shop, where skilled Artificers, working with ancient Implements, supply many of the unusual Requirements of the *Restoration*, while exemplifying and explaining their Crafts to Visitors.

AND, though they are not owned by the *Restoration* Corporations, it should also be noted that the complete Restorations of *Bruton Parish* Church and of the Powder Magazine (owned by the *Association for the Preservation of Virginia Antiquities*) were accomplished in this Period, the Work for the most Part being contributed by 'Mr. *Rockefeller* to the Institutions concerned—even as the *Sir Christopher Wren* Building, the President's House, and *Brafferton* Hall were restored for the College of *William and Mary* in the opening Years of the *Restoration*.

MOREOVER, new Buildings have been added in the Business Area of the City; and great Advances have been made in the Provision of Accommodations for the Visitors from every Section of the Country and from all Parts of the World who are attracted to *Williamsburg* in ever-increasing Numbers. Two large Hotels have been erected on the Border of the Restoration Area, and a Number of restored or reconstructed Taverns, Ordinaries, and Dwelling Houses have been associated with these in the Reception and Entertainment of Guests. These lesser Buildings, for the most Part, are thus returned to the Purposes which they served originally when, during colonial Publick Times, the City was no less crowded than at the Present.

ALSO, in this Period, the *Restoration* has entered upon a Programme for the Promotion of Crafts, through which it hopes to extend the Influences of its Buildings and their Furnishings, as well as those of the Period and Civilization represented. In this Endeavor carefully selected and accredited Manufactories, working under the Supervision of *Restoration* Experts, are reproducing countless Selections from the Collections and decorative Materials of the *Restoration*, and are making these available for Publick Purchase both in *Williamsburg* and throughout the Country.

MORE recently, as the Restoration has begun to approach its enlarged and final Form, new and added Emphasis has been placed upon the Means and Methods of its Interpretation. Surveys by Authorities in the Field of Education are now in Progress. Endeavors in historical Research, at first directed principally to the Provision of Information requisite for physical Restoration, have been broadened to permit extensive Studies in the general Field of *English-American* colonial History and its social, political, economic, and religious Pertinences—with particular Emphasis laid upon the History of *Virginia* and of *Williamsburg*. Nor are such Endeavors confined wholly to *Restoration* Agencies, for in late Months a limited Number of Fellowships have been granted to certain well-qualified Scholars desiring to pursue and publish Studies concerning *Williamsburg* in the eighteenth Century, and the Origin, Development, and Expansion of the Civilization of which the City was the Center. It is intended that the published Results of such Studies will supplement the more extensive Endeavors of the several Departments of the *Restoration* and the Publications issued by them. And the Information thus attained will in Time become diffused in the common Knowledge, to the End that *Williamsburg* (which has been advanced herein as a City which, through a strange Coincidence of History, was all but forgotten) will resume its rightful Place in the History of *Virginia* and, thence, in the History of the Country at large.

So it is, then, that the *Restoration* faces the Future at the Time of this Writing. And, though the Future is not the proper Province of an historical Report, it may be said with considerable Assurance that so, with slowly changing Emphasis, it will continue. As the physical Restoration approaches its attainable Limits, with a consequent Dwindling of structural Activity, interpretative and educational Activities will undoubtedly increase and multiply. A substantial Number of additional Buildings of the eighteenth Century will likely be restored and reconstructed; for Plans for certain such Additions have already been completed, and Plans for yet others are in Preparation. Doubtless additional Exhibition Buildings will be opened to the Publick from Time to Time, until a fair Representation of the early domestic, institutional, commercial, and industrial Life of the Community is rendered against a significant and enhancing Background.

Toward and for the Fulfillment of these Possibilities and Probabilities of the Future, an Organization of some seven Hundred and fifty Persons, working in fourteen specialized Departments or Divisions, is now employed. And it is of Interest to note that this Organization is soon to have its *Williamsburg* Headquarters in a new Structure, to be known as the *Goodwin* Building—

named in Honour of Mr. *Rockefeller's* first Associate in the *Williamsburg Restoration*, who died on *September* 7, 1939, after forty Years of tireless Work, in *Bruton* and other Parishes of his Church, for the Strengthening of the Spirit of Man and the Enrichment of human Life and Understanding.

✿ ✿ ✿

AT the Close of so unparticular a Discourse concerning the *Williamsburg Restoration* the Reader may be curious concerning the Purposes of the Project and the Ends it will seek to attain.

AND in Answer to so involved a Question it can only be explained that in its Composition the *Restoration* has many Phases and Spheres which offer many Interests and Appeals. By some the Spaces and Gardens of *Williamsburg* will be looked upon merely as Settings for the Architecture of its Buildings. To others the Buildings will appeal chiefly as Backgrounds for these Spaces and Gardens. Some may be attracted to the restored City as to a great Repository for Art and Antiquities. Others may seek it as a Center of pure Learning—of Dates, and Manuscripts, and scholarly Research. And it is hoped that each may find some Value and Enjoyment.

BUT for the *Restoration* itself, for the Donor and those who have worked for the Fulfillment of the Endeavor, the Hope is this: That the *Williamsburg Restoration* will, in each of its Spheres and Phases and through them all, revive and retain

Something of the Strength and Beauty of another Age, Something of the Spirit of the Men who lived in it and made it great; that it may say of them as *Pericles* said of the *Athenian* Dead:

" *So they gave their Bodies to the Commonwealth,*
" *and received, each for his own Memory, Praise*
" *that will never die; and with it the grandest of*
" *all Sepulchres, not that in which their mortal*
" *Bones are laid, but a Home in the Minds of Men,*
" *where their Glory remains fresh to stir to Speech*
" *or Action as Occasion comes. For the whole*
" *Earth is the Sepulchre of famous Men; and their*
" *Story is not graven only on Stone over their*
" *native Earth, but lives on far away, without*
" *visible Symbol, woven into the Stuff of other*
" *Men's Lives.*"

FINIS.

The

INDEX.

A.

*A*ccomac County, 8, 9.
  Actors, 35.
Acts of Assembly, 3, 12, 27.
  for building Capitol, 15, 19, 21.
  for building Palace, 23.
  for building *Williamsburg*, 15, 19, 21, 22.
  for seating *Middle Plantation*, 2-3.
Adams, John, 54.
Albemarle County, 65, 78.
Aldermen, 30, 46, 84.
America, 18, 24, 49, 61, 68, 72, 78, 95. SEE ALSO *English-America*, *North America*.
American Folk Art, 117.
American Revolution, 52, 53-54, 63, 74-83, 85, 106.
  Causes of, 53.
  Outbreak of, 70, 71, 72.
American Troops, 80, 81, 82, 83.
Ammunition, 25, 93.
Amsterdam, 31.
Andros, Sir *Edmund* (Gov.), 28.
Animals, 86.
Antiquarians, 112.
Apothecaries, 35.
Apothecary's Shop, 86.
Appomattox, Surrender at, 90.
Apprentices, 103.
Archæological Exhibit, 117.
Archæology, 98. SEE ALSO *Wil-*

(Archæology, cont'd.)
  liamsburg Restoration, archæological Work.
Archer's Hope Creek, 3, 19.
Architects, 100, 101, 108, 113, 115, 116, 118, 119.
  advisory, 101.
Arms, 10, 25, 70, 71.
Army, *American*, 81, 83.
  British, 83.
  Confederate, 87.
  SEE ALSO Troops.
Arnold, Benedict, 80.
Artificers, 30.
Artillery, 82.
Artisans, 103, 116.
Artists, 110.
Asia, 48.
Assembly, SEE General Assembly.
Association for the Preservation of Virginia Antiquities, 93, 100, 120.
Atlantic Ocean, 111.
Attorneys, 35.
Attorneys General, 44, 51.
Auctions, 75.
  of Slaves, 37.
Augusta County, 65.

B.

*B*acon, *Nathaniel*, 6, 7, 8, 9, 10, 11.
  Commission of, 7, 9.

C.

Cabinet-makers, 35.
  Cabinet-maker's Shop, 120.
Cables, 93, 99.
Caesar, 51.
Canada, 48.
Canals, 29.
Candles, 60.
Capitals (*Virginia*). SEE *James-town*, *Richmond*, *Williams-burg*.
Capitol (*Williamsburg*), 37, 42, 52, 74, 84.
  Act for building, 15, 19, 21.
  at *Middle Plantation*, 15.
  Bell at, 84.
  Botetourt Statue at, 62.
  Building of, 22.
  Burning of, (1747), 45, 111. (1832), 85.
  completed, 24.
  Description of, 29.
  eastern Half demolished, 85.
  first used, 24.
  Foundations preserved, 98.
  Furnishing of, 110-111.
  Land for, 21.
  Piazza of, 62.
  Prison near, 77.
  Rebuilding of, 45.
  Reconstruction of, 110, 111, 116.
  Repairs to, 85.
  Rooms in, 111.
  Site of, 93, 98.
  Theatre near, 45.
Capitol Square, 102.
Carpenters, 35.
Carr, Dabney, 66.
Carter, Robert, 32.
Cartographers, 106.
Cary, Archibald, 74.
Cattle, 2.
Cattle-stealing, 5.
Cedar, 30.
"*Cerberus*," 72.
Chairmakers, 35.
Chaises, 30.
Chandlers, 35.
Chaplains, 29.
Chariots, 30.
Charles I, 51.
Charles II, 8, 10, 12.
Charles River County, 3.

Charters, of College, 13, 40.
  of *Virginia* Company, 47.
  of *Williamsburg*, 84.
Cherokees, Emperor of, 47.
Chesapeake Bay, 3, 8, 18.
Chickens, 91.
Chimney Caps, 99.
Chorley, Kenneth, 119.
Church Fairs, 87.
Churches, 25, 92.
  at *Middle Plantation*, 13, 19, 24.
  SEE ALSO *Bruton Parish* Church.
Cipher, *W & M*, 20.
Cities, 11, 17, 78. SEE ALSO Towns.
Civil War, 87-90, 113.
Clark, George Rogers, 76.
Clayton, Polly, 60.
Clergy, 28.
Clergymen, 13.
Clerks, 35.
Cloaks, 75.
Clocks, 91.
Cloth, 65.
Coaches, 30, 37, 58, 60.
Coachmakers, 35.
Coats, 57.
Cockmatches, 37.
Coleman, George P., 91.
College, at *Henrico*, 14.
College of William & Mary, 21, 22, 35, 37, 94.
  Aid to, 91.
  Arts & Sciences at, 40.
  Assembly meets at, 22.
  at *Middle Plantation*, 13, 19.
  Bell at, 84.
  Blair, first President, 28.
  Blair promotes, 13.
  Botetourt buried at, 62.
  Botetourt Statue at, 62.
  Brafferton Building at, 41, 121.
  Building of, 14.
  Burning of, (1705), 24. (1859), 87. (1862), 89.
  Chancellor of, 43.
  Chapel of, 62.
  Charter for, 13, 40.
  Description of, 29.
  Divinity School at, 40, 41, 43.
  Endowments for, 13.
  Exercises suspended, 91.
  Faculty of, 40, 41. SEE ALSO Pro-fessors at.
  Fires at, 24, 87, 89, 98.
  Foundations laid, 13-14.

G.

Gambling, 50.
Game, 90.
Gaols. SEE Prisons, Public Gaol.
Garages, 98.
Gardeners, 35.
Gardens, 29, 30, 90, 105, 113, 114, 115, 117, 118, 124.
English, 114.
Southern, 114.
Garner's Store, 99.
Gasoline Stations, 94.
Gates, 29, 107.
Geldings, 83.
General Assembly, 2, 7, 9, 12, 13, 15, 19, 20, 21, 23, 25, 32, 36, 38, 39, 45, 46, 49, 50, 52, 57, 59, 61, 66, 67, 72, 73, 75, 85, 110, 111.
at Capitol, 24.
at College, 22.
at Middle Plantation, 11-12.
Botetourt dissolves, 59.
Botetourt Statue ordered by, 62, 63.
Fauquier dissolves, 52.
fourteen Year Assembly, 7.
Taxation by, 27, 51, 59, 73.
SEE ALSO Council, House of Burgesses.
General Congress. SEE Continental Congress.
General Court, 36, 38.
George I, 26.
George III, 51, 55, 61, 74.
Germans, 45.
Glaziers, 35.
Glisters, 86.
Gloucester, William, Duke of, 20.
Gloucester County, 9.
Goldsmiths, 35.
Gooch, William (Lt. Gov.), 32, 45, 46.
Administration of, 32-33, 34.
Letter of, 38.
Resignation of, 44.
Goodwin, Rev. William A. R., 92, 94, 99, 124.
Goodwin Building, 123.
Gordon, Lord Adam, 34.
Governor's Palace, 37, 38, 70, 77.
Act for building, 23.
Ball at, 38-39.
Basement of, 107.

(Governor's Palace, Cont'd.)
Botetourt at, 62.
Burning of (1781), 85, 89.
Canal at, 29.
Cellars of, 107.
Completion of, 24.
Cupola of, 29.
Description of (1724), 29.
Dunmore at, 68-69.
Dunmore flees from, 72.
Entertainments at, 29, 37-38, 39.
Floor Plan of, 105.
Foundations excavated, 107-108.
Furniture in, 110.
Gardens of, 29, 105, 107.
Gates of, 29, 107.
P. Henry at, 75.
Hospital in, 83.
Jefferson's Floor-plan of, 105.
Lands of, 85, 105.
Mantelpieces of, 107.
Offices of, 29, 89-90, 105, 107.
Outbuildings of, 107.
Picture of, 105.
Reconstruction of, 105, 116.
Repairs to, 45, 47.
Standing Furniture in, 110.
Steps of, 107.
Theatre near, 26, 45.
Walks of, 29, 107.
Walls of, 107-108.
Wells of, 107.
Wine Bins of, 107.
Governors, 44, 64, 108.
Deputies of, 56.
House for, 47.
SEE ALSO Andros, Berkeley, Botetourt, Dinwiddie, Drysdale, Dunmore, Fauquier, Gooch, Harvey, Hunter, Jefferson, Jeffreys, Nicholson, Nott, Spotswood, Wyatt.
Granby, Lord, 57.
Grand Assembly. SEE General Assembly.
Great Britain, 18, 20, 31, 40, 53, 56, 66, 69, 71.
Peace with, 83.
War with France, 49.
Green Spring, 10.
Gunpowder, 70.
Payment for, 71.
Removal of by Dunmore, 70.
Guns, 56, 80.
Gunsmiths, 35.

H.

Hadley, Thomas, 14.
Hairdressers, 35.
Hamilton, Henry, 76, 77.
Hams, 86.
Hand, General, 82.
Hangings, 10.
Hanover, 38.
Troops from, 71.
Hansford, Charles, 57.
Harnessmakers, 35.
Harrison, Benjamin, 21, 43, 68.
Harrop Parish, 4.
Harvard College, 14.
Harvey, Sir John, 2, 5.
Hatpins, 110.
Hats, 65.
Hatters, 35.
Head of Elk, 83.
Henrico, University at, 14.
Henry, Patrick, 51, 66, 71, 74.
Appearance of, 75.
at Governor's Palace, 75.
Commander of Virginia Forces, 73.
Delegate to Congress, 68.
Governor, 75, 76, 77.
Speech of, 51, 68, 69.
Henry Street, 20.
Heralds, 83.
Higginson, Capt. Robert, 4, 5.
Hill, General, 88.
Historians, Committee of, 101.
Historical Societies, 105.
Horse-races, 37.
Horses, 37, 58, 75.
Horseways, 19, 20.
Horticulturists, 115.
Hose, 65.
Hospitals, at College, 83.
at Palace, 83.
in Williamsburg, 83, 88.
Hotels, 121.
House of Burgesses, 21, 48, 51, 56, 73, 74, 111.
Chaplain to, 29.
Day of Fasting appointed by, 67.
final Session, 73.
Resolutions of, (1769), 59.
(1773), 66.
SEE ALSO Burgesses.
House of Commons, 50.
House of Delegates, 75.
House of Representatives, 44.
Hunter, Robert, 24.

I.

Illinois, 47.
Illuminations, 29, 39, 68, 76.
Indiana, 47.
Indians, 1, 2, 26, 40, 47, 76.
at College, 40, 41, 42.
Cherokees, 47.
Massacre by, (1622), 1, 6, 14.
(1644), 4.
Murders by, 7.
Peace with, 12.
Trade with, 7, 47.
Treaties with, 12, 47.
War against, 7, 8, 9.
Inns, 30, 36. SEE ALSO Ordinaries,
Publick Houses, Taverns.
Insurance Policies, 105.
Inventories, 110, 111.
Ireland Street, 20.
Irish Potatoes, 86.
Irish Servants, 30.
Iron, 107.

J.

Jailers, 35, 77.
Jails. SEE Prisons, Public Gaol.
James City, 2.
James City County, 25.
Court House for, 25.
James River, 2, 3, 19, 81.
Plantations on, 2.
Jamestown, 2, 3, 6, 78, 81.
burned by Bacon, 9, 10.
burning of Statehouse, 14.
County Seat moved from, 25.
in Ruins, 11.
Seat of Government moved from, 15.
Statehouse at, 12, 15.
Jefferson, Thomas, 42-43, 49, 66, 92.
Declaration of Independence by, 54.
Floor-plan of Palace by, 105.
Governor, 77, 105.
Jeffreys, Herbert (acting Gov.), 11, 12.

[133]

[141]

The Days of Men grow long and short
  With constant Repetition;
Likewise the Length of this Report
  Has varied—each Edition.